Cecilia Magnusson Sjöberg (ed.)

IT Law for IT Professionals
– an introduction

G000024668

Studentlitteratur

Art. No 31895
ISBN 978-91-44-03736-3
Edition 1:3

© The authors and Studentlitteratur 2005
www.studentlitteratur.se
Studentlitteratur AB, Lund

Cover design by Pernilla Eriksson

Printed by Holmbergs i Malmö AB, Sweden 2010

Contents

Foreword

The modern information society calls for networking in many regards. New technical infrastructures in combination with globalisation of organisations give rise to legal considerations of a variety of kind. To mention just a few current issues that will be addressed in this book:

- How can you legally protect intellectual property rights on the Internet?
- Under what circumstances is it possible for an employee to claim copyright to program code developed at the working place?
- When is a bid published on the website of an international e-marketplace binding as an offer as opposed to being conceived of as an invitation to treat?
- What are the major pitfalls associated with e-procurement in comparison with conventional procurement methods?
- What are the preconditions for an electronic signature to be legally valid?
- Does e-invoicing from a legal point of view require electronic identities associated not merely to a legal person but to a specified natural person?
- What kind of alternative dispute resolution may be resorted to in an Internet environment?
- Why may illegitimate personal data processing turn out to be a true economic risk in spite of low levels of damage?
- How can law help in balancing IT-related challenges to fundamental principles of freedom of information and expression?
- How can e-government be used from a business point of view and what are the major rights of an individual being subject to automatic legal decision making by a public authority?
- How is one to deal with risks for non-legal actions associated with business activities on the Internet given the fact that criminal law traditionally is tied to national jurisdictions?

Clearly, the introduction and use of information and communications technology has a great impact on private sector as well as public sector activities. A book of this kind, however, cannot provide full and precise answers to all the questions enumerated above. In fact the legal situation of today's information society is such that it is not feasible to deliver generally applicable analyses of IT law issues without taking the factual circumstances (including jurisdictional ones) surrounding a certain case into consideration. What can be accomplished, though, is a growth of understanding of the kind of legal issues that call for attention when, for instance, doing business using web technologies.

The quest for deepened legal awareness is also the overall goal of two introductory IT law courses. One is offered to students at the Stockholm University Department of Computer Science. The other one is part of an international master programme of informatics and security organised by the Royal Institute of Technology (KTH), Stockholm, in co-operation with the University. In addition to the request to come up with suitable literature within my Course-Director role, my ambition as editor of this book is that it will prove valuable to IT professionals in general. Given the high level of expertise and experiences of IT law in practice represented among the contributing authors, it is my belief that this goal can be met. In addition I would like to express special thanks to Christine Kirchberger, Lecturer in the University, for assisting me in the editing process. Additionally it should be mentionell that this textbook was produced with financial support from the Stockholm University Law Faculty Publishing Trust and the Awapatent Foundation for the promotion of Scientific research in the area of intellectual property rights.

Finally, there is much to benefit from legal awareness at early stages of system design and development. Legal customisation of already implemented technical applications is in principle cost intensive, i.e. if it is at all possible to accomplish legally well-founded solutions at a later stage. There is no doubt a strong business imperative to try to prevent legal trouble that may result in court proceedings. Legally initiated IT professionals working together with representatives for the legal domain will definitely support the much-needed proactive approach to IT law.

Cecilia Magnusson Sjöberg
Stockholm, January 2005

1 Introduction to law in a digital environment

Cecilia Magnusson Sjöberg

1.1 Law and IT

Computerisation has wide-ranging legal implications. In a historical perspective law has developed with a focus on physical objects locatable within the national sovereignty of a particular legal system. Well-known social developments towards a constantly growing number of activities based on the use of information and communications technology without geographical boundaries have fundamentally changed these conditions. In many respects it is a true challenge to transpose prevailing legal rules and methods for problem-solving into an environment characterised by immaterial resources. The legal community is successively taking up new roles in the shaping of law, and these new roles will be the point of departure in this introductory chapter.

Let us to begin by very briefly touching on what law is all about. Generally speaking, law functions as an instrument when things have already gone wrong. A well-known example of this is judicial assessments by courts deciding cases as well as alternative dispute resolutions. Furthermore, law-making bodies commonly react to activities in society by taking legislative measures. Law may also come around as a proactive approach stating beforehand, in rules and regulations, what is legally acceptable and/or prohibited. Contracts of different kinds may basically have the same effect between the parties involved.

In the context of the digital information society, there is in fact a growing need for proactive law. This, bee it noted, does not imply a request for more legislation. On the contrary, a proactive legal approach to IT emphasises the need for early integration of legal aspects in system design and development. In addition to benefits on an individual basis, legally well-founded IT applications in society will on the whole reduce the incentive for law-making bodies to issue the kind of detailed provisions that very few actors on the information market appreciate.

The dimension of proactive law in digital environments may be further illustrated by the fact that e-government in the form of automatically generated administrative legal decisions, for example within the areas of social insurance and taxation, is based on transformations of legal rules into algorithms that can be executed by computers. This transformation of legal information into program code represents in itself a kind of proactivity, because the fixation of law in the form of computer programs will be decisive for all the forthcoming legal decision making based on that automatic procedure. Another example of a new kind of proactive legal activity concerns applications of information standards, e.g. vocabulary design for e-business transactions.

These two examples of law being developed outside conventional legal frameworks illustrate the need for an early introduction of a legal perspective. One question then arising is what the basis for such a legal perspective would be in terms of overall goals and means of measuring whether the end result meets fundamental legal requirements. In addition to well-known goals of best business practices, cost efficiency, etc. "the rule of law" is an expression that can be said to capture what generally is to be deemed as a good legal solution. There exists, however, no formal definition of what is to be understood by the rule of law and different legal systems have their own expressions given their national context.[1]

A legal system based on democratic values commonly associates the rule of law with (a) forseeability, (b) uniformity and (c) openness. It is important to note that the notion of forseeability should not be conceived of as a right for individual parties to be able to predict the exact outcome of a pending case. Forseeability rather indicates a basic right of knowing what legal principles and rules that will form the basis for a court verdict or state agency decision.

---

1   For example "Rechtssicherheit" in Germany and "rättssäkerhet" in the Scandinavian countries.

Furthermore, uniformity being an inherent aspect of the rule of law implies that similar cases should be treated on an equal basis. However, it might very well be necessary to take the individual factors surrounding each case into consideration and also, for instance, local variations due to geographical circumstances. For instance, going by taxi transport for a medical appointment might be refundable within a social insurance system for a patient living in the countryside where there is no public transport available, but not for someone living in the city.

Openness in the rule of law context refers primarily to transparency in public sector activities. The character of a principle of openness – if at all existing – varies a lot between different jurisdictions. In some, publicity is the major rule and secrecy is the exception, and in others it is quite the opposite. An important distinction has to be made between a regulatory framework laying down that it is a public agency's own choice to disseminate information, and rules making it mandatory to hand out documents on the request of someone representing the general public. Principles of openness are often manifested in a nation's fundamental laws, given the importance of openness for efficiency control and for preventing corruption. In the IT era, principles of openness have come to serve yet another purpose. More precisely, private enterprises are increasingly availing themselves for commercial reasons, such as direct marketing, of data collected and stored by public authorities. Here, obviously, we have a potential conflict of interest between freedom of information and privacy protection.[2]

There are many different roles in working life helping to preserve the rule of law. Those of the judge, attorney-at-law, case-handling official and academic are familiar. In addition to these established legal professionals, there are contract managers, providers of legal information services, designers of e-business applications and legal decision support systems, and many more who in their daily working life are involved in law without any formal legal training.

The approach to a working agenda including legal issues may differ considerably depending on which legal system is at hand. Without entering in any detail into this question, attention may be

---

2   See further Chapter 2 in this volume: Kirchberger, Christine, *Freedom of information and privacy protection.*

11

drawn to the fact that there can be said to exist two major kinds of legal system. One is conventionally referred to as the common law system and the other as the civil law system. Legal developments in national jurisdictions adhering to common law, e.g. the British and American ones, will primarily depend on judicial decisions. In a civil law system, which may be exemplified by central Europe and the Scandinavian countries, emphasis is instead placed on how law is laid down in rules and regulations issued by law-making bodies. In both systems, however, cases as well as written rules play an important role.

In addition to a need to differentiate between the common law system and the civil law system, a borderline has to be drawn between public and private law. Although these sectorial areas of society are not as distinct as they used to be, due to the impact of IT-based networking and data exchange in general, the two fields do have different regulatory frameworks. In practice this affects, for instance, system design in that there are generally many more legal rules to take into consideration, i.e. administrative law, when developing a decision support system for a public agency[3] as opposed to IT-based knowledge management within, for instance, a private business law firm. To a large extent it boils down to competence and authority to deal with legal information and the kind of sanctions that unauthorised activities may result in.

It follows that those involved in legal system design must be aware of the wide variety of information types representing law. To mention just a few, there are rules and regulations of different norm-hierarchical status, preparatory works reflecting the history of law-making, decided cases by courts and public authorities, standard contracts as well as individually shaped ones, legal doctrine and commentaries. Legal information is not just any kind of information, because document types have different formal status (to some extent depending on the legal system at hand). When, for instance, coding legal information for the purpose of future decision-making, binding rules as opposed to non-binding recommendations on how to interpret and apply law should not be treated in the same way. Furthermore, the legal profession is quite sensitive as regards conventions for referencing etc. Keywords attached to a precedent (i.e.

---

3   Conditions for e-government will be dealt with in Chapter 3, below.

meta data) will only be acknowledged if they have been inserted by someone with the authority and competence to do so.

Infrastructural changes lead to new conditions for developments in society, which is basically why there is a need to study the inter-action of law and information technology. More precisely, there are two major lines of interest when addressing law and IT. One con-cerns substantive law issues of how to interpret and apply legal rules and regulations in a digital environment, which is of primary inter-est in this book. The other has to do with methods for legal man-agement of information systems. The major incentive for investi-gating this is that IT applications often represent great values and also may have an impact on the rule of law (see above). The need for legal advice in this context boils down to the importance of being aware of predominant legal principles already when architecturing e-solutions. In practice, though, it is not meaningful to entirely sep-arate between these two focal points of material law on the one hand and legal system management on the other.[4] As an introduc-tion to forthcoming chapters this will be illustrated by a brief dis-cussion about electronic signatures used for legal purposes.

There is no doubt that electronic signatures and other means of secure electronic messaging are becoming established in society. The main question of law in relation to this development is whether, how and to what extent electronic signatures can be given the same legal effect as handwritten ones. As already indicated, the aim here is not to provide a detailed analysis of these questions in the light of different jurisdictions.[5] At this stage it is sufficient to state that law-governing activities among parties in the private sec-tor of society in general are surrounded by a relatively limited number of formal requirements concerning handwritten signa-tures. Typical examples where such signatures are in fact required include consumer credits and real-estate purchases. In family law, testamentary dispositions and marital property agreements are not valid without handwritten signatures. In administrative law it is more common to require signing, since processing of cases often presupposes submission of signed documents.

---

4   See further Magnusson Sjöberg, Cecilia (ed.), *Legal management of information systems: incorporating law into e-solutions*, Studentlitteratur, Stockholm, 2005.
5   "Legal potentials and pitfalls of electronic signatures" are treated in depth by Anna Nordén in Chapter 8.

The implementation of the EC Directive on a Community framework for electronic signatures (1999/93/EC) clarifies certain aspects with regard to legal acceptance of digital signing. The overall objective of this EC Directive can be said to be co-ordination of the legal and technical work of the European Union member states, so as to remove the obstacles to the internal market, especially as regards e-commerce. The EC Signature Directive contains provisions relating to the legal effects of electronic signatures and the organs that may prove capable of offering electronic certificates verifying the genuineness of such signatures.

However, there is still a lot of work to be done before e-transactions can be performed on a daily basis in a sufficiently secure way. In spite of rapid developments in many regards there still remains a need to minimise uncertainties as regards both different legal issues and practical (partly technical) circumstances surrounding electronic handling of documents. It may also be pointed out that business models and administrative traditions have not yet been fully adapted to the potentials of electronic document management.

As a result of regulatory approaches such as the above mentioned EC Directive, electronic signatures under certain circumstances have been granted legal enforceability, which was not the case earlier in those countries which lack the principle of free examination and evaluation of evidence.

In an attempt to extract some general principles – or rather indications – of legal validity of electronic signatures, the following may be concluded. When the legislator uses a term like "written", electronic communication may be allowed to take place. At the same time a requirement of written procedure is posited by such a wording as opposed to oral procedure. When a statement contains expressions such as "signature", or "that must be signed by the party in question", or the like, then this does not necessarily mean that electronic documents or electronic signatures may be allowed to replace traditional paper documents and manual signatures. However, special rules or established practice may permit the use of electronic form after all.

As regards evidentiary value of an electronic signature, the state of law depends on whether the jurisdiction in question is characterised by the principle of free examination of evidence (see above). In general terms such a framework for court proceedings means that there are no limitations on the sources of evidence that may be used in a trial, and also that a judge is not bound by any special regulations regarding the way in which different types of evidence shall be evaluated. Another aspect worth mentioning in this context has to do with rules on the burden of proof, which could be dependent on the medium used in a given case. Without such procedural rules, evidential assessments will instead be based on the parties´ internal relations, the character of the legal documents in question, etc. Under those circumstances, i.e. when there are no formal obstacles to a court considering system evidence in the sense of electronic documents, electronic signatures and other components of information systems, the payback for early legal awareness during system design will show.

1.2   IT more than a tool

1.2.1   Legal document management and information standards

Sticking to documents as a basis for a discussion about IT being more than a conventional mechanical tool might appear somewhat old-fashioned. But for all the growing impact of multimedia on the legal domain, the document concept is central as a basis for legal investigations of different kinds, above all because law is still produced in the form of text entities captured in the form of documents. Common legal document types are, as already mentioned, acts and ordinances, case law, contracts and clauses, conventions and so forth. Actually, a more appropriate expression in this context would be virtually tangible documents meaning that these kinds of objects representing law may occur in electronic as well as in paper formats. The introduction and application of information technology has, furthermore, led to a state of affairs where the boundaries of a particular kind of legal document are not necessarily defined beforehand.[6]

---

6   The Swedish principle of publicity, for instance, is characterised by a right of access to dynamic constellations of data. Under the Freedom of the Press Act, Chapter 2, Section 3, a so-called recording for automatic data processing is deemed held by a public authority if available to the authority using technical aids, which the authority itself employs.

Within the field of IT-supported legal document management there is a growing need for version control in a long-term perspective. Document markup, including linking techniques of different kinds, is attractive as a general value-adding method. At the same time, the introduction and widespread use of more and more advanced digital document management systems are generating complex environments for text handling. Furthermore, a major trend in today's communication networks is open systems. One important concern, therefore, is how best to secure trails of authorisations, alterations included. More precisely, this is a matter of information security policies mirroring the norms that govern an organisation, such as who has the right of access to what, without knowing beforehand who will be claiming this right of availability.

Regulatory management may here serve as an illustration of an application area in demand for IT support. The rapid growth of legal norms in general and the internationalisation of law as such[7] have put information standards in focus. Considering that the major characteristics of normative documents are complex, interdependent text units shifting in content over time, interpretable only in context, we can extract one key issue, and that is the need for a methodological approach. The cornerstone in such a method of modern regulatory management would be in particular structured documents and information security. Information standards naturally represent a major method as regards structured documents. More precisely, the W3C recommendation XML (Extensible Markup Language)[8] offers vital possibilities of transparent modularity in a structural context. As regards information security it here denotes the conventional set of factors comprising in particular availability, authenticity, (data) integrity, confidentiality (secrecy), accountability and non-repudiation.

Although this book is intended for readers with knowledge of IT, a brief presentation of document markup from a legal point of view will perhaps not be altogether out of place. The focus of attention will be on the need for and potentials of a dynamic approach to legal

---

7   In Europe, for instance, the incorporation of new member states into the European Union gives rise to legal harmonisation activities and transpositions of EC Directives etc. into national law.
8   See further http://www.w3.org/XML/.

text handling, beyond flat representation of keywords attached to the beginning of a document or search words inserted in an (inverted) text file.

A markup language may be used to represent structures and contents, styling and communications. This implies that not only the core XML W3C Recommendation is of interest for the legal domain, but also related standardisation initiatives such as XSL (Extensible Stylesheet Language), SOAP (Simple Object Access Protocol), etc. Bearing this in mind, XML ought to be regarded as a symbol for a system development approach commonly including data management in terms of text handling.

At the beginning of the relatively short history of markup languages was SGML (Standard Generalized Markup Language), an ISO standard dating back to 1986.[9] In the legal domain there are still many running applications based on SGML – legal publishing, for instance. At one stage of development the SGML community was a pretty closed one, not particularly amendable to discussions concerning the pros and cons of various database technologies, etc. Today the situation has changed in that XML[10] can be said to play a central role in more or less any technical solution involving web technologies, telecommunications as well as conventional electronic data processing and to some extent also techniques having their origin in artificial intelligence.

All of this may no doubt be elementary to the already experienced user of information standards. Practical experience has shown, however, that a common misunderstanding at the management level of an organisation, be it a private enterprise or a public agency, is that XML (in a broad sense) used for legal information management involves adhering to a particular type of system design and possibly even software product. Representatives of the industry (including IT professionals) thus have the educational task of explaining the underlying ideas of a non-proprietary approach to data

---

9   ISO 8879:1986.
10   Formally a true subset of SGML but benefiting from the more easy-to-use aspects of HTML (Hyper Text Markup Language), for instance, by not requiring the use of a so-called DTD (Document Type Definition). In comparison with HTML, an important difference is that while HTML aims at presentation of text on a (computer) screen, a major purpose of XML is to allow for semantic expressiveness. Furthermore, the HTML DTD consists of a predefined tag set whereas an application based on XML is open to any kind of customised vocabulary.

management. Otherwise there is an obvious risk that such a lack of understanding may turn out to be a major obstacle to widespread use of information standards in the legal domain.

In fact there are considerable legal advantages to be gained from awareness of the inherent capacities of XML. Thus the choice of system development approach as such may have an impact on a court's assessment, for instance, of whether an organisation's archival system is to be regarded as accurate or negligent in terms of meeting legal requirements of evidence by keeping track of version-dependent legacy data. The pharmaceutical and motor industries are typical examples of branches heavily burdened by legal demands for documentation. However, it may not be a trivial task in a litigation situation to explain to a court how the use of information standards within a particular IT-application manifests a party's legal awareness.

An XML document may be well formed or governed by a DTD (Document Type Definition) or schema. A DTD defines the composition of a set of documents (e.g. laws, court cases and contracts). It contains information about document elements (court instance, parties' involved, legal issue at stake, verdict, date of decision, etc.) and the logical order of these elements and their frequency, etc. A DTD is expressed in XML and may be stored in a data file outside the document.

There are different ways of explaining the underlying meaning of a DTD. One could focus on the purpose of a method of structured information description in context. This implies that a DTD does not necessarily have to be related to a certain type of document but rather to some particular kind of information. A skilfully designed DTD with corresponding markup makes it possible to adjust the use of particular document to a variety of intentions, i.e. without having to change the markup. XML then plays the role of an enabling method, making it possible, for instance, to find information that is of relevance on a specific occasion. This is an indication of how important a preparatory (legal) document analysis is.

A schema can be generally described as a specification or formal definition of the constraints on the content of an XML document, aiming at both structure and functionality. One way to specify a schema is to use a DTD, but XML schemas can model other kinds of structured data as well and are in principle more expressive. An important feature of an XML schema is the possibility of integrating database functionality and communication between applications. A major purpose of an XML schema is indeed to make it support data typing (integer, date etc.) and thereby facilitate XML data interchange with conventional database systems. XML schemas are written in XML and have been developed for use on internet and are therefore co-ordinated with other W3C specifications.

In the simple example below of a document instance, element tags and attributes with their value are displayed in bold characters. The value of attribute tag ID is shown in the "article tag". "A3-95-46-EC" here stands for Article 3 in the EC Data Protection Directive.

Of the utmost importance, not the least from a legal point of view is the inherent validation component of an XML application governed by a DTD or schema. In practice this means that a marked-up document is validated against the predefined logical constraints (such as decided order of elements) and the predefined number of particular elements.

```
<ARTICLE ID = ´A3-95-46-EC´>
<ARTITLE> Scope </ARTITLE>
<ARTNO> Article 3 </ARTNO>
<PARA> 1. This Directive shall apply to the processing of personal data wholly or partly by automatic means, and to the processing otherwise than by automatic means of personal data which form part of a filing system or are intended to form a part of a filing system. </PARA>
...
</ARTICLE>
```

So far so good, but is the XML approach secure and what makes it all worth investigating in terms of legal implications? One starting point is that legal document management requires co-ordination in order to meet demands for efficient production, supply and use. Apart from general needs to improve recall and precision when retrieving legal information, there is also reason to consider, for instance, knowledge management attempts and exchange of business data in networks of various kinds.

When using markup languages for legal document management it is important to note that interpretations and (strategic) decisions on structural components may have a bearing on law itself. This is even more the case when markup goes beyond structure into mirroring contents, as this hardly can be done in a complete objective manner. Merely by adding that a precedent, for instance, addresses a certain legal principle and therefore would be of relevance for the understanding of another (court) case is to be regarded as a subjective statement of law. Yet another example of this kind of non-trivial legal data processing might be the insertion of hypertext links indicating connections between subordinate and governing superior rules. In fact the mere styling of legal text entities in terms of bold, italics etc. could represent unauthorised manipulation of the underlying legal information.

Information standards have a potential to function as a lever of and a sound basis for all of these development needs in the legal domain. In this context it should be mentioned that information standards applied have a profound impact on substantive law itself, in particular in the fields of contract law, intellectual property rights and privacy protection. To exemplify, XML messaging quite often comprises personal data processing in a legal sense (cf. EC Data Protection Directive 95/46/EC). It concerns the requirements of consent from data subjects to collect, store and disseminate personal data. Furthermore, modern e-business models make it necessary to consider information duties, e.g. that the identity of a service provider must be clarified according to the EC Directive on E-commerce (2003/31/EC). Liability issues are also relevant in terms of analysing who is responsible for damage emerging as a result of the abuse of a transferred authentication.

Generally speaking, it all boils down to trust in global digital information and a need for legal information security in open as well as closed computer-based networks. Every organisation needs to reflect upon the handling of documents governing internal as well as external actions. One highly important question, for example, is how far information standards may support message authentication and electronic measures to prevent distortion of (document) content. The concept of authority here covers a wide variety of actions, e.g. authorisations to enter into contract and law enforcement.

Who, then, in practice would benefit from legally secure use of information standards? To begin with, secure use of XML is relevant for commercial actors as well as for representatives of the public sector. This can be instanced with buyers who, in a procurement situation, are dependent on clarification of legal conditions governing a particular situation. In a vendor perspective, the use of a legal checklist may be regarded as a business opportunity in terms of legally founded security branding of offered solutions. Enhancing legal awareness among politicians and public officials for the purpose of efficiency, forseeability, uniformity, openness, etc. is another obvious advantage.

1.2.2   XML-related security enhancing factors

This section will illustrate how structured documents accomplished by means of standardised markup languages may be regarded as a freeway route on the map of an information society characterised by security. The overall goal may be expressed in terms of trusted public and business activities in the context of information retrieval, knowledge management, automated decision-making, e-commerce, etc. Trust implies information security conventionally comprising the criteria of availability, confidentiality (secrecy), integrity, accountability and non-repudiation. Clearly, these building bricks of information security have legal implications as regards system design and management as well as concerning applicable rules and regulations.

The discussion above may be summarised in terms of a need for a strategy to handle legal uncertainty characterising today's digital society. In practical terms this manifested need may be transformed to a focus on XML related security enhancing factors. The table below presents an overview – not an exhaustive list – of what are here referred to as XML characteristics, means and legal incentives. The overall purpose is to illustrate a legally oriented approach to information security based on applied IT, i.e. information standards.

Table 1.1 IT as a means for security enhancement in the legal domain.

1. XML characteristics	2. Means	3. Legal incentives
Non-proprietary format	Inherent in any XML application	Public sector: Accessibility in a long-term perspective Private sector: Legal requirements of keeping track of legacy data
Quality assurer in document production	Validated documents by means of DTD:s and schemas	*Public sector:* Public information supply (possibly state responsibility) *Private sector:* Commercial products (avoiding liability)
Quality assurer in document distribution	One single repository as a basis for custom-ising production, e.g. CD-ROM, on-line, print	*Public sector:* See above *Private sector:* See above
Container of legal directives	Markup vocabularies	*Public and private sectors:* – Availability differentiator e.g. whether official or secret data? – Authority indicator e.g. mirroring acting parties authorities – Property rights administration e.g. labelling rights and its owners
Secure electronic messaging	For instance, XML Signatures and/or mathematically based approaches to incremental signa-tures of structures and marked-up documents	*Public and private sectors:* Normative as well as other legal requirements of authenti-cation, validation and signed documents (text entities)

1.2.3 Summing up

We have now seen how information standards may be regarded as a means for accomplishing legally valid proof of actions in a security context. A point is made of the fact that XML ought to be under-stood broadly and that the tool metaphor has implications beyond trivial physical and mechanical ones. XML has instead strong infrastructural potentials closely interlinked with IT-support for information retrieval and automatic legal decision making. From a legal point of view, this deserves particular attention.

The fact that there are still so many legal uncertainties in terms of lack of forseeability concerning formal legal validity of actions of various kinds calls for special attention. A pragmatic approach has been presented in terms of regarding various characteristics associated with information standards as security enhancing factors. The attraction of combining XML with a conventional approach to information security methods lies in the need for transparent, content-dependent and context-sensitive management of legally relevant text units over time.

1.3 Changing legal infrastructures

The summing up of this introductory chapter will be made by way of pointing to certain changes in legal infrastructures. The term infrastructure is often used to describe the fundamental functions of society. It can refer to both "hard infrastructures" such as the road system, broadband etc. or "soft infrastructures", such as social systems and various types of information systems. The basic components of a legal infrastructure,[11] which may be regarded as "soft" according to the above-mentioned classification, include various forms of (a) data processing, (b) documentation, (c) communication, and (d) organisation forms.

The introduction and use of information and communications technology in society has dramatically changed all these components. For example, data processing within the public sector, which used to be manual in the past, was transformed step by step during the 1970s and 1980s into automated processing of case data. Today, automation of administrative activities, in the sense of legal decision-making based on wholly or partly automated routines, can be termed a characteristic feature of administrative procedures and an aspect of e-government. Another type of computerised legal data

---

11 The notion of legal infrastructure may be explained as those parts of a legal system that forms the basis and conditions for legal activities.

processing takes place in connection with the framing and conclusion of contracts. E-contracting with the whole world as a market place calls for a discussion of fundamental legal principles underlying offers, acceptance, evaluation of evidence, etc. Information standards obviously have a role to play here as means of improved legal system management, considering their potential for handling version-dependent text units over time.

Earlier generations of lawyers would naturally associate the concept of "documentation" with physically demarcated paper documents, which would be geographically located. In the age of the Internet this view is no longer valid. Instead electronic documents are carriers of declaratory acts, proprietary rights, criminal contents, etc. Information standards clearly mirror this development. Mention should here be made of such initiatives as XML Signatures that explicitly address the need for incremental signatures, which, for instance, may be of relevance in a situation of successive drafting of contracts.

In a similar way (voice-based) analogical communication services are being used less frequently in legal work. Both civil servants' communications with citizens and lawyers' contacts with their clients are increasingly dependent instead on digital and mobile services.

As regards organisational forms there is commonly a legal tradition of working with nationally well-demarcated larger and smaller entities. This is especially clear as regards the information system of public administration, which has often developed in harmony with nationally defined government authorities divided into central and local agencies, etc. Information technology as such and the internet as a concept have provided leverage for loosening up/dissolving boundaries between authorities as well as national demarcation lines. The private sector can be said to be characterised by even more all-embracing network-based and global organisation forms in recent years.

2 Freedom of information and privacy protection

Christine Kirchberger

Information technology not only affects everybody's daily life, it also influences different balances struck in a legal system. Occasionally, new techniques and the possibilities created by them can tilt this balance, e.g. businesses can utilise personal data collected from their customers in order to adapt marketing very efficiently. In other circumstances, the individual might gain from an increased access to public information due to the automation of public processes and a larger amount of data being stored.

Two areas where information technology has had quite a large impact are privacy protection and freedom of information. In fact the question of conflicting interests is quite complex in that it concerns balancing both between the areas of privacy protection and freedom of information versus security as well as between privacy protection and freedom of information. Is this always the case or can you actually take on an anonymous shopper's role? In both fields the balance between different interests is especially important and legislation has to take new technological possibilities into account.

2.1 Privacy

When ordering a book from an online shop, you are required to reveal some personal data, such as your name, address, telephone number, e-mail address and so forth. This information is necessary in order to enable the delivery of the book, to guarantee payment and to facilitate communication with you in case of a problem.

Sometimes the online company also asks you to register as a customer and to state special interests, hobbies, your birthday etc. This information allows the seller to send you further advertising or special offers for your birthday or for other occasions.

These are example of how personal data is being used nowadays in order to enable or encourage e-business. In addition, public authorities are processing data about citizens when dealing with tax issues or social benefits for example.[1]

In all these cases, data about a certain person is being collected, transferred organised, stored, used, spread or changed. Generally speaking, the aim of existing privacy legislation[2] is to identify whether or not a person's privacy is at risk and to what extent. Businesses have an interest in collecting and using personal data in order to become more efficient in their marketing strategies. "Data are commodities."[3] On the other hand, individuals have an interest that their personal data is not used in ways that violates their privacy. It is up to legislation to stipulate rules in order to find the balance required.

2.1.1 Concept of privacy

Privacy as such can be either physical or psychological.[4] Physical privacy would include protection against bodily violence of any sort, e.g. injuries, kidnapping, murder. Psychological privacy has a less clear description, but can be said to focus on the intangible part of integrity that affects personal integrity, e.g. a newspaper taking a picture of a person and publishing it in its next issue or – a less intrusive example – somebody collecting the names and addresses of persons passing by.

In this chapter the emphasis will be on psychological privacy. The terms used in legislation differ from country to country, though *privacy* seems to be the key term mostly mentioned.[5] Within the Euro-

---

1   *See* Chapter 3 in this volume: Magnusson Sjöberg, Cecilia, *E-government.*
2   For instance the EC Data Protection Directive serves the purpose of supporting the internal market.
3   Blume, Peter, *Data Protection in the Private Sector*, in Wahlgren, Peter (ed.), *IT-Law*, Scandinavian Studies in Law, Volume 47, Stockholm Institute for Scandinavian Law, Stockholm, 2004, pp. 299–300.
4   Blume, Peter, *Data Protection in the Private Sector,* p. 298.
5   Bygrave, Lee A., *Privacy Protection in a Global Context – A Comparative Overview*, in Wahlgren, Peter (ed.), *IT-Law*, Scandinavian Studies in Law, Volume 47, Stockholm Institute for Scandinavian Law, Stockholm, 2004, p. 320.

pean Union the term *data protection* is widely spread, mostly due to the fact that the major legal basis uses this expression. Other concepts invoked are *freedom, liberty* and *autonomy, la vie privée* (French), *die Privatsphäre* (German), *personlig integritet* (Sweden).[6] Another more recent term that serves as a bridge between European and North American discussions is *data privacy*. All these terms stand, however, for the same idea, which is a person's private sphere, his or her personal integrity. It should be mentioned here that an enterprise's need for private sphere conventionally is not protected by privacy legislation.

The concept changed over time. Living in a small village in the Middle Ages meant that most people knew each other, each other's names, addresses, hobbies, family relationships. In small communities privacy might be different than in a large city, where most people are anonymous to each other. IT made everybody more visible again. When you buy a book in a shop the salesperson does not need to know your name if you pay cash. If you order a book over the Internet, you have to state your name, address, credit card number, etc. Due to the technical framework, anonymity is less possible than in the offline world.[7] This change did not happen over night, but since the dawn of the Internet and more and more entities doing business online, questions of identification arose and how to secure the payment for purchased products. This lead to an increase in personal data being processed.

There are different ways to define privacy. The theories range from non-interference, i.e. the right "to be let alone," to information control, i.e. one person's ability to decide which information should be available to whom.[8] There is, however, no single definition of privacy, as the concept differs from culture to culture, country to country, time to time and person to person.

> "To the extent that a panhuman need for privacy exists, this appears to be rooted not so much in physiological or biological but social factors. [...] However, technological-organisation factors are not the sole

---

6   Bygrave, Lee A., *Privacy Protection in a Global Context – A Comparative Overview*, pp. 320–321.

7   *See further* Lessig, Lawrence, *Code and other laws of cyberspace*, Basic Books, New York, 1999.

8   For a more detailed analysis *see* Bygrave, Lee A., *Privacy Protection in a Global Context – A Comparative Overview*, p. 323.

determinants of privacy levels. Also determinative are ideological factors. Central amongst there are attitudes to the value of private life, attitudes to the worth of persons as individuals, and sensitivity to human beings' non-economic and emotional needs."[9]

The main aim of data protection legislation is to establish rules in order to ensure that personal data are not used in ways that can violate personal integrity. Most of the different statutes or international agreements do not define the concept, but rather focus on defining what type of processing is allowed and what requirements it is subject to. This Chapter will deal with the main international agreements and specifically with European Union legislation, which will serve to exemplify the different principles of data protection. As an illustration, certain national law will be mentioned as well.

2.1.2   International agreements

The right to privacy is one of the fundamental human rights granted by various international treaties and national legislation. Human rights constitute the basis of democracy and guarantee every individual fundamental rights, such as the right to life, the right to integrity of the person, prohibition of torture and inhuman or degrading treatment or punishment, prohibition of slavery and forced labour. Originally human rights protected the citizens against the state. This is very visible in the following prerogatives: right to an effective remedy and a fair trial, the presumption of innocence and the right of defence, principles of legality and proportionality of criminal offences and penalties, the right not to be tried or punished twice in criminal proceedings for the same criminal offence.[10] Certain human rights, such as the right to privacy, have, however, moved from affecting only the relation between public authorities and the citizen towards influencing as well the relations between individuals or between individuals and private entities.

---

9   Bygrave, Lee A., *Privacy Protection in a Global Context – A Comparative Overview*, pp. 327–328.

10   *See e.g.* Article 11 of the Universal Declaration of Human Rights: (1) Everyone charged with a penal offence has the right to be presumed innocent until proved guilty according to law in a public trial at which he has had all the guarantees necessary for his defence.

One of the first international agreements concerning human rights was the Universal Declaration of Human Rights[11], adopted in 1948 by the Member States of the United Nations General Assembly.[12] The Declaration as such is not legally binding, though it has engendered more than 60 human rights instruments, including the International Covenant on Economic, Social and Cultural Rights and the International Covenant on Civil and Political Rights. Both these treaties are legally binding, which means that the signatory states face legal consequences if they do not implement and adhere to these rules.

The Universal Declaration of Human Rights states in Article 12:

> No one shall be subjected to arbitrary interference with his privacy, family, home or correspondence, nor to attacks upon his honour and reputation. Everyone has the right to the protection of the law against such interference or attacks.

Another international treaty that protects privacy as a human right is the European Convention on Human Rights, drawn up by the Council of Europe in 1950.[13] At the moment 46 countries have signed the convention, 45 of which have ratified it.[14] The Convention has the advantage of being equipped with an enforcement mechanism that enables individuals to pursue the rights granted them by the Convention. The European Court of Human Rights[15] was created in 1959, and any individual or any Contracting State can file a complaint directly, claiming infringement by a Contracting State of any of the rights granted by the Convention.

---

11 http://www.un.org/Overview/rights.html.
12 At that time the United Nations General Assembly had 58 Member States. The countries included Afghanistan, Argentina, Australia, Belgium, Bolivia, Brazil, Burma, Canada, Chile, China, Colombia, Cuba, Egypt, India, Iran, Iraq, Lebanon, Liberia, Luxembourg, Mexico, Netherlands, New Zealand, Nicaragua, Norway, Pakistan, Panama, Paraguay, Peru, Philippines, Sweden, Syria, Turkey, United Kingdom and United States. More information at http://www.unhchr.ch/udhr/miscinfo/carta.htm.
13 European Convention for the Protection of Human Rights and Fundamental Freedoms, as amended by Protocol No 11, http://www.echr.coe.int/Convention/webConvenENG.pdf. Some background information can be found at http://www.coe.int/.
14 http://conventions.coe.int/.
15 http://www.echr.coe.int/.

Article 8 (Right to respect for private and family life) states

1 Everyone has the right to respect for his private and family life, his home and his correspondence.

2 There shall be no interference by a public authority with the exercise of this right except such as is in accordance with the law and is necessary in a democratic society in the interests of national security, public safety or the economic well-being of the country, for the prevention of disorder or crime, for the protection of health or morals, or for the protection of the rights and freedoms of others.

The Council of Europe also initiated the first internationally binding instrument, the Convention for the Protection of Individuals with regard to Automatic Processing of Personal Data[16] in 1981. Other examples of international instruments, though not legally binding, are the OECD Guidelines on the Protection of Privacy and Transborder Flows of Personal Data, adopted in 1980 and the 1998 Ministerial Declaration on the Protection of Privacy on Global Networks.[17] In this context the United Nations Guidelines for the Regulation of Computerized Personal Data Files should be mentioned as well.[18]

These international agreements and guidelines form the basis of national legislation often with constitutional character, and EC lawmaking. The principles stipulated in the mentioned regulations are visible in different national statutes and national laws, and especially in the EC Data Protection Directive, which is why the Directive will serve to exemplify the basic legal concept of data protection.

2.1.3 EC Data protection regime

In addition to granting every individual a fundamental right of privacy[19] the European Union has regulated certain processing of personal data in several directives. The most important of these would

---

16 ETS No 108.
17 http://www.oecd.org/dataoecd/39/13/1840065.pdf.
18 Resolution 45/95, adopted by General Assembly 14 December 1990, http://www.unhchr.ch/html/menu3/b/71.htm.
19 Article 7 – Respect for private and family life: "Everyone has the right to respect for his or her private and family life, home and communications." Charter of fundamental rights of the European Union (2000/C 364/01).

seem to be the Data Protection Directive[20] and the Directive on Electronic Communication[21].

EC Directives have to be implemented in national law, i.e. they are not directly applicable to the extent that a citizen of a Member State can have recourse to the European Commission or the European Court of Justice[22] and claim rights stipulated in a directive. This is possible under specific circumstances but not the general rule.[23] National legislation is therefore, in principle, still required in order to give legal effect to the principles laid down a directive. Nevertheless, the national lawmakers have to legislate within the framework of the directive.

The Data Protection Directive is not applicable in the field of public security, defence and criminal law (Article 3 (2)), which leaves parts of the public sector out of this legislation. This does not imply that public authorities can gather and store personal data as much as they want. It simply means that the Data Protection Directive cannot be applied. Registries and databases held by public authorities are very often regulated by specific legislation in which the rights and obligations are stated in detail.

Historically, the main objective of the Data Protection Directive has been to ensure the free flow of personal data between the Member States. With the development of the European Union into more than an economical organisation, another objective, to protect the fundamental right of privacy, has become more and more important.[24] These aims are achieved by granting the individual certain rights when it comes to personal data and by creating legal requirements that have to be followed when entities process personal data.

---

20 European Parliament and Council Directive 95/46/EC of 24 October 1995 on the protection of individuals with regard to the processing of personal data and on the free movement of such data [Data Protection Directive].

21 Directive 2002/58/EC of the European Parliament and of the Council of 12 July 2002 concerning the processing of personal data and the protection of privacy in the electronic communications sector [Directive on privacy and electronic communications].

22 http://www.curia.eu.int; Not to be confused with the European Court of Human Rights, http://www.echr.coe.int/.

23 One of the court cases that has laid down some principles concerning "direct effect" of EC directives is The Court of Justice of the European Communities, C-6/90, Judgment of 19/11/1991, Francovich and Bonifaci / Italy (Rec. 1991, p. I-5357).

24 *See* Article 1 Data Protection Directive.

Furthermore, each Member State has to establish a supervisory authority, i.e. a public authority responsible for monitoring the application of data protection legislation.[25] The Directive has been implemented in the diffrent Member States by national instruments and regulations.[26]

The Electronic Communication Directive focuses more on the communications sector and stipulates different obligations for electronic communication providers with regard to personal data. In many national legal systems telecommunication service providers have to follow specific regulations when it comes to processing of data related to the communication service as such.

2.1.4 Basic notions of data protection

In order to fully understand the legal regime on data protection some terms and concepts have to be explained. Again, the definitions from the Data Protection Directive may serve as an example, considering that the concepts are similar in several countries.

2.1.4.1 Personal data

The "object" of regulation is personal data. Before looking at the requirements and principles of data protection, one has to establish whether the data in question constitutes *personal data*.

Article 2 (a) of the Data Protection Directive (Data Protection Directive) defines personal data as *any information relating to an identified or identifiable natural person ('data subject'); an identifiable person is one who can be identified, directly or indirectly, in particular by reference to an identification number or to one or more factors specific to his physical, physiological, mental, economic, cultural or social identity.* Examples include a name, an address, a telephone number, a social se-

---

25 Article 28 Data Protection Directive. Examples are the Swedish Data Protection Board (Datainspektionen, http://www.datainspektionen.se), for the UK The Office of the Information Commissioner (http://www.dataprotection.gov.uk) or the Austrian Data Protection Commission (Datenschutzkommission des Bundeskanzleramtes, http://www.dsk.gv.at/).

26 An overview over different national legislation on privacy protection, both within the European Union and outside, can be found at http://www.privacyinternational.org/. Concerning EU initiatives and material see http://europa.eu.int/comm/internal_market/privacy/index_en.htm.

curity number, a picture, audio and film recordings, an IP number, an e-mail address, DNA, fingerprints, etc.

According to Recital 26 of the Data Protection Directive "to determine whether a person is identifiable, account should be taken of all the means likely reasonably to be used either by the controller or by any other person to identify the said person". In other words, even the e-mail address mickymouse@mail.com can be considered personal data as long as the owner of the address stated his/her real name when registering the account, as in this case "any other person" has the means to identify the owner. The same seems to apply for IP numbers, as it is possible for the Internet Service Provider even in the case of a dynamic IP address to link the IP number to a certain person (the subscriber). The same argument can be used in order to regard encrypted data as "personal data" as long as somebody can decrypt the data.

So, to sum up, as long as any party, not necessarily the controller, can link certain data to an identifiable individual, it can be considered personal data.[27] This concept is applicable to several legal systems.

2.1.4.2 *Processing of personal data*

"Processing of personal data ('processing') shall mean any operation or set of operations which is performed upon personal data, whether or not by automatic means, such as collection, recording, organization, storage, adaptation or alteration, retrieval, consultation, use, disclosure by transmission, dissemination or otherwise making available, alignment or combination, blocking, erasure or destruction."[28]

Processing is therefore more or less any handling of personal data. Each type of processing has to be carried out according to the principles of data protection and fulfil all requirements. This means, e.g., that when an online company is gathering information about its customers, each step in the course of action has to comply with data protection legislation. One can imagine a scenario where the

---

27 Kuner, Christopher, *European Data Privacy Law and Online Business*, Oxford University Press, New York, 2003, p. 51.
28 Article 2 (b) Data Protection Directive.

collection of the personal data, as well as the storage of it, is legitimate under the legislation; the dissemination of the personal data might, however, violate the data protection rules and therefore be forbidden.

Simple storage of personal data on any medium, such as a hard drive, a USB memory or a server, is already considered processing. In other words, personal data does not have to be stored in a larger database or edited in any way in order to fall under data protection legislation. As soon as the data is digitalised, it is being processed.

It is clear that the means of processing have improved immensely since the dawn of information technology. When documents where handled in written form, processing meant that one person was writing a document or filling out a form and this form was then sent to a clerk at the authority. Nowadays more data is stored in one place, and data can be accessed and spread a lot faster, and involve more people.

2.1.4.3 Controller

The person or entity, either public authority or private company, duty bound to follow the data protection rules is called *controller*. According to Article 2 (d) of the Data Protection Directive *'controller' shall mean* "the natural or legal person, public authority, agency or any other body which alone or jointly with others determines the purposes and means of the processing of personal data".

2.1.5   When processing is allowed

The Data Protection Directive is applicable when personal data is processed wholly or partly by automatic means (Article 3). Manual files can be included in the Data Protection Directive if they "form part of a filing system". This means that the (manual) filing system is structured in a way that allows specific information about a certain person to be accessed easily. Examples for such manual filing systems would be filing cabinets and card index boxes where the data is ordered by name of the person.[29]

---

29   Chissick, Michael & Kelman, Alistair, *Electronic Commerce: Law and Practice*, 3rd ed, Sweet & Maxwell, London, 2002, p. 211.

According to Art 3 (2) the Directive shall *not* apply to processing of personal data "by a natural person in the course of a purely personal or household activity". Therefore, private address books stored on the computer or on the mobile phone, even if they contain pictures, do not fall under the Data Protection Directive.[30]

A personal homepage however, cannot be considered private activity in accordance with Art 3 (2). From Recital 12 of the Data Protection Directive the conclusion can be drawn that *personal activity* relates to a closed personal or domestic circle and not providing information to anyone anywhere in the world, which is the case when publishing data on a webpage.[31]

Any other processing of personal data not intended for private purposes only, has to be allowed based on one of the conditions presented below:

2.1.5.1 Consent

The most common ground for legitimate processing of personal data is the consent of a data subject in accordance with Article 7 (a). This means that the individual agrees to the processing. According to Article 3 (h) *the data subject's consent* shall mean "any freely given specific and informed indication of his wishes by which the data subject signifies his agreement to personal data relating to him being processed."

The consent therefore has to be:

*   free
*   specific
*   informed
*   and has to signify the intent

Free can be interpreted as voluntary, i.e. the individual has the choice of agreeing or not agreeing to the processing. This might not be as easy to establish at it seems. If a person does not agree to the

---

30 See also Recital (12) of the Data Protection Directive.
31 See Paragraph 47 in Judgment of the Court of 6 November 2003, Criminal proceedings against Bodil Lindqvist, Case C-101/01. *See also* (as the Court decision is not available in English) the Opinion of Mr Advocate General Tizzano, delivered on 19 September 2002, Case C-101/01, at Paragraph 34.

privacy terms of an online business, the only choice left might sometimes be not to become a customer. In employment situations the conditions for a *free consent* might be different as well. An example could be that the employer intends to monitor all e-mails and all web traffic of the employees. Depending on his or her position in the company, an employee might not have any choice but to consent.

Specific indicates that the expression of will has to concern a certain processing in a certain situation by a certain controller for a certain purpose.[32] *Informed* means that the data subject has to be given information about the intended processing of his or her data, prior to the consent.

An example that does not seem to fulfil the requirement of specific and informed would be "Hereby you consent to the processing of your personal data for marketing purposes". Marketing purposes is rather vague in this context.[33] In order to comply with privacy legislation, the data controller should state in detail what data is collected, how it is being used (e.g. storing of which information, dissemination of which details, etc.) and if the data is shared with third parties. Online companies commonly state their privacy principles in the General Terms and Conditions, which leads to the risk that customers registering might not be aware of the privacy policy. It is debatable whether a privacy statement "hidden" in the General Terms and Conditions fulfils the requirement of *informed*. Contract law can be of help when it comes to deciding to what extent the user agreed to certain terms, depending on if they were hidden or unexpected.[34]

When it comes to online services, the establishment of certificates and agreements has become more and more common. In order to be able to use a certain certificate on its website, the organisation has to adhere to certain requirements. One example would be TRUSTe®, an independent non-profit organisation that tries to establish trust for online business especially with regard to personal

---

32 Ehmann, Eugen, Helfrich, Marcus, *EG Datenschutzrichtlinie – Kurzkommentar*, O. Schmidt Verlag, Köln, 1999, p. 88.
33 Chissick, Michael & Kelman, Alistair, *Electronic Commerce: Law and Practice*, p. 214.
34 See Chapter 6 in this volume: Ramberg, Christina, *Designing a legal interface for contracting on the Internet*.

integrity.[35] In order to become a TRUSTe®-licensed site, the entity must provide on their website:[36]

A privacy statement, including the following disclosures:

- What personal information is collected and how it will be used
- Identity of the party collecting personal information
- Whether personal information is shared with third parties
- The use of any tracking technology
- Whether personal information is supplemented with information from other sources
- Choice options available to consumers
- How consumers can access personal information they have provided
- That there are security measures in place
- Procedures for filing and addressing consumer complaints

In addition, the privacy statement must:

- Be linked from the home page and from every page where personal information is collected
- Bear the TRUSTe "Click to Verify" link so consumers know whether the company is a TRUSTe licensee or not

In order for the consent to be *signified,* some form of active communication is required from the individual.[37] The data subject cannot be considered to "signify his or her agreement" if the controller only assumes that the individual consents, i.e. *hypothetic consent* is not sufficient. In other words, an online company cannot send out an e-mail to its customers announcing that it will create a large database with its customers' names, addresses, hobbies and previous purchases of and assume that every customer agrees to this processing of personal data. Some sort of expression of will by each customer is necessary in order for the consent to be legitimate under data protection legislation. *Tacit consent*, i.e. no statement whatsoever, is not sufficient either. Signified consent does, however, not necessarily include the specific statement "Yes, I agree to the processing of my

35 http://www.truste.org/about/mission_statement.php.
36 http://www.truste.org/requirements.php.
37 Chissick, Michael & Kelman, Alistair, *Electronic Commerce: Law and Practice*, p. 214.

personal data". In some cases it can be acceptable, if the action of the individual indicates consent.[38] An example would be that a person is asked to submit personal data while being informed about the processing that will take place, and he or she simply submits the personal data.

The consent does not have to be in written form, an oral expression of somebody's will is sufficient. For evidence purposes, however, and depending on the type of personal data being processed, it might be important to safeguard documentation of a given consent.

2.1.5.2   Other situations where data processing is legitimate

According to Article 7 of the Data Protection Directive, data processing can also be allowed if the individual has not given his or her consent under the following circumstances:

b) processing is necessary for the performance of a contract to which the data subject is party or in order to take steps at the request of the data subject prior to entering into a contract; or

c) processing is necessary for compliance with a legal obligation to which the controller is subject; or

d) processing is necessary in order to protect the vital interests of the data subject; or

e) processing is necessary for the performance of a task carried out in the public interest or in the exercise of official authority vested in the controller or in a third party to whom the data are disclosed; or

f) processing is necessary for the purposes of the legitimate interests pursued by the controller or by the third party or parties to whom the data are disclosed, except where such interests are overridden by the interests for fundamental rights and freedoms of the data subject which require protection under Article 1 (1).

An example for (b) performance of a contract could be somebody buying a book from an online bookstore. The company has to know

---

38   In the Swedish legal system this concept is called *konkludent handling*, in German and Austrian legislation *Schlüssige oder konkludente Willenserklärung*. A proper translation could be "conclusive statement".

the name, address, and billing information in order to be able to send the book and charge the buyer the price.

Examples for legal obligations could be that companies have to comply with tax and social security legislation,[39] e.g. inform the tax authority about the tax deducted from the salaries of their employees. In order to fulfil its tax-law obligations, the company has to process data about its employees.

A person's vital interests could be at stake if they are brought to the hospital, unconscious. In this case the hospital can process data about them, even if the data subject is not able to consent at that moment.

Different authorities, such as tax authorities, municipalities or other administrational authorities, even universities, have to process personal data in the line of *exercising official authority*. If the tax authority is processing a tax declaration, it is naturally processing personal data as well. This, however, is legitimate, even if the data subject does not consent.

The interpretation of "legitimate interests" in (f) is a bit uncertain. Recital 30 of the Directive mentions the processing of personal data "in the context of the legitimate ordinary business activities of companies and other bodies" and the possibility for the data subject to object to such processing.[40] One could assume that simple marketing measures, such as sending e-mails with special offers, are possible, as long as the customer does not object. It is worth mentioning here that if the privacy statement is included in the General Terms and Conditions, the individual agreeing to the conditions also consents to the processing of the personal data and therefore the processing is legitimate, based on the consent and not on a weighing of interests.

---

39 Kuner, Christopher, *European Data Privacy Law and Online Business*, pp. 59.
40 "Member States may similarly specify the conditions under which personal data may be disclosed to a third party for the purposes of marketing whether carried out commercially or by a charitable organization or by any other association or foundation, of a political nature for example, subject to the provisions allowing a data subject to object to the processing of data regarding him, at no cost and without having to state his reasons."

2.1.5.3 Special categories of data

If the personal data concerns a person's racial or ethnic origin, political opinions, religious or philosophical beliefs, trade-union membership, or the health or sex life, special regulations apply.[41]

Article 8 of the Data Protection Directive stipulates the principle that such data shall not be processed, unless specific circumstances justify the processing. These circumstances include:

a) the data subject has given his explicit consent to the processing of those data;[42] or
b) processing is necessary for the purposes of carrying out the obligations and specific rights of the controller in the field of employment law; or
c) processing is necessary to protect the vital interests of the data subject or of another person where the data subject is physically or legally incapable of giving his consent; or
d) processing is carried out in the course of its legitimate activities with appropriate guarantees by a foundation, association or any other non-profit-seeking body with a political, philosophical, religious or trade-union aim and on condition that the processing relates solely to the members of the body or to persons who have regular contact with it in connection with its purposes and that the data are not disclosed to a third party without the consent of the data subjects; or
e) the processing relates to data which are manifestly made public by the data subject or is necessary for the establishment, exercise or defence of legal claims.

Moreover, processing of sensitive data is allowed where it is "required for the purposes of preventive medicine, medical diagnosis, the provision of care or treatment or the management of health-care services, and where those data are processed by a health professional subject under national law". Also the processing of data "relating to offences, criminal convictions or security measures may be carried out [...] under the control of official authority."

---

41 Article 8 Data Protection Directive.
42 The Directive states "explicit consent" which means that the requirements are a bit higher than for a "normal" consent.

Another *special category of data* could involve traffic data, i.e. data that are processed for the purpose of the conveyance of a communication on an electronic communications network or for the billing thereof.[43] These data include details about time, place and numbers used for fixed and mobile voice services, faxes, e-mails, SMS and other use of the Internet. The main idea is that communication providers are allowed to process traffic data to the extent the storage and processing is necessary for billing purposes or for the communication as such.[44] The data should not be kept longer than necessary, in accordance with the principles stated below. In the context of cybercrime and criminal activities over the Internet, public law enforcement agencies very often have an interest in accessing traffic data in order to trace the intruder or perpetrator. Especially after 9/11, lawmakers and politicians are requesting more possibilities for data retention in the "fight against terrorism".[45] Communication providers, on the other hand, very seldom want to keep traffic data longer than necessary as they fear that their customers will loose trust in the service and furthermore the storage of large amounts of data costs money.[46]

2.1.6 Principles of data protection

Article 6 Data Protection Directive stipulates the principles that controllers have to adhere to when processing data. This means that processing data not only has to be allowed based on certain grounds, but controllers also have to follow certain guidelines when processing data.

---

43 Definition in Article 2 (b) Directive on privacy and electronic communication.
44 Article 6 Directive on privacy and electronic communication.
45 See e.g. eGovernment News, *ICT to play a crucial role in Europe's fight against terrorism,* 29 March 2004, EU & Europe-wide, http://europa.eu.int/idabc/en/document/2342/5654; concerning the United States *see* Office for Homeland Security, http://www.whitehouse.gov/homeland/.
46 *See e.g.* World Information Technology and Services Alliance (WITSA), *Background Paper on Traffic Data Requirements and Cooperation with Law Enforcement Authorities,* November 2004,
   http://www.witsa.org/papers/DataRetention-final.pdf.

Article 6

1 Member States shall provide that personal data must be:
   (a) processed fairly and lawfully;
   (b) collected for specified, explicit and legitimate purposes and not further processed in a way incompatible with those purposes. Further processing of data for historical, statistical or scientific purposes shall not be considered as incompatible provided that Member States provide appropriate safeguards;
   (c) adequate, relevant and not excessive in relation to the purposes for which they are collected and/or further processed;
   (d) accurate and, where necessary, kept up to date; every reasonable step must be taken to ensure that data which are inaccurate or incomplete, having regard to the purposes for which they were collected or for which they are further processed, are erased or rectified;
   (e) kept in a form which permits identification of data subjects for no longer than is necessary for the purposes for which the data were collected or for which they are further processed. Member States shall lay down appropriate safeguards for personal data stored for longer periods for historical, statistical or scientific use.

2 It shall be for the controller to ensure that paragraph 1 is complied with.

2.1.6.1 Data shall be processed fairly and lawfully

Personal data has to be processed in accordance with Article 7 of the Data Protection Directive. In other words, either the data subject has consented to the processing or the processing is allowed based on one of the other rules previously mentioned.

2.1.6.2 Data shall be obtained for specific and legitimate purposes

The purpose of the data processing has to be clear and specified before the data is being processed. This means that the controller has to specifically inform the data subject about the purposes for which the data are being collected or stored or otherwise processed.[47]

In addition, after the personal data were collected, the purpose cannot be changed afterwards without notifying the data subject or

---

47 Kuner, Christopher, *European Data Privacy Law and Online Business,* p. 60.

the Data Protection Authority. In other words, any further purpose must not be incompatible with the original purpose.[48]

A non-legitimate purpose can be instanced with a website publishing the e-mail address of users participating in an online discussion forum.[49] "Spyware"[50] can also be considered as having no legitimate purpose.[51]

2.1.6.3 Personal data shall be adequate, relevant and not excessive

Personal data shall be adequate, relevant and not excessive in relation to the purpose for which the data are to be processed. An online company, for example, shall not collect more information than necessary. If a potential customer registering at a website is asked to state marital status, salary, hobbies, etc., the webpage should indicate which fields are obligatory and which are voluntary.[52]

2.1.6.4 Personal data shall be accurate and, when necessary, kept up to date

Data controllers have to take "reasonable steps" in order to ensure that the data are accurate and up to date. This also depends on the purpose for which the data were obtained or processed.[53]

---

48 *Ibid.*, p. 60.
49 *Ibid.*, p. 61.
50 Spyware is "software that covertly gathers user information through the user's Internet connection without his or her knowledge, usually for advertising purposes. [...] Because spyware exists as independent executable programs, they have the ability to monitor keystrokes, scan files on the hard drive, snoop other applications, such as chat programs or word processors, install other spyware programs, read cookies, change the default home page on the Web browser, consistently relaying this information back to the spyware author who will either use it for advertising/marketing purposes or sell the information to another party." http://www.webopedia.com/TERM/s/spyware.html.
51 "As these technologies are by definition used without informing the user (the name spyware speaks for itself) they are a form of invisible and not legitimate processing." Art.29 Data Protection Working Party, Working document on determining the international application of EU data protection law to personal data processing on the Internet by non-EU based web sites, 30 May 2002 5035/01/EN/final, WP 56, p. 12.
52 Kuner, Christopher, *European Data Privacy Law and Online Business*, p. 61.
53 *Ibid.*

2.1.6.5 *Personal data shall not be kept for longer than is necessary*

Periodic data audits should be carried out in order to determine if the data have to be kept or deleted.[54]

2.1.6.6 *Security of processing*

In order to ensure data protection, data controllers have to take appropriate technical and organisational measures according to Article 17 Data Protection Directive:

> Member States shall provide that the controller must implement appropriate technical and organizational measures to protect personal data against accidental or unlawful destruction or accidental loss, alteration, unauthorized disclosure or access, in particular where the processing involves the transmission of data over a network, and against all other unlawful forms of processing.
>
> Having regard to the state of the art and the cost of their implementation, such measures shall ensure a level of security appropriate to the risks represented by the processing and the nature of the data to be protected.

In this respect standardisation plays an important role, also with regard to the principle of "purpose limitation", i.e. personal data shall only be "collected for specified, explicit and legitimate purposes and not further processed in a way incompatible with those purposes". This principle leads to the concept of "data minimisation" which means that the amount of personal data processed should be kept to the minimum necessary. Furthermore, privacy enhancing technologies[55] contribute to data minimisation.[56]

One attempt for such standardisation is the Initiative for Privacy Standardization in Europe (IPSE), which was established by the European Standards Bodies CEN[57], CENELEC[58], and ETSI[59]. The

---

54 Chissick, Michael & Kelman, Alistair, *Electronic Commerce: Law and Practice*, p. 216.
55 See below, Sub-chapter 2.1.7.
56 Kuner, Christopher, *European Data Privacy Law and Online Business*, p. 196.
57 European Committee for Standardization, http://www.cenorm.be/.
58 European Committee for Electrotechnical Standardization, http://www.cenelec.org/.
59 European Telecommunications Standards Institute, http://www.etsi.org/.

project issued a report in September 2000 on the question of standardisation in the field of data protection.[60]

Due to the fact that Article 17 is rather vague and does not define "appropriate technical and organizational measures", it is up to the Member States and especially the Supervisory Authorities to regulate more specifically on the level of security. The Information Commissioner's Office in the UK issued some guidelines concerning security measures in the private sector. In this paper, the British Supervisory Authority expressed the view that "appropriate will depend on the circumstances, in particular, on the harm that might result from, for example, an unauthorised disclosure of personal data, which in itself might depend on the nature of the data. The data controller, therefore, needs to adopt a risk-based approach to determining what measures are appropriate. Management and organisational measures are as important as technical ones. Standard risk assessment and risk management techniques involve identifying potential threats to the system, the vulnerability of the system to those threats and the countermeasures to put in place to reduce and manage the risk."[61]

Measures that should be taken into consideration include security management (e.g. a clear security policy), control of access to information (e.g. access to the buildings, passwords, procedures for authenticating the identity of a person) and detecting breaches of security (audit trails, logging, investigation of breaches).[62]

2.1.6.7   Transfer of personal data to a third country

A transfer of personal data to a country outside the European Union or the European Economic Area (the EEA)[63] is only allowed if the third country "ensures an adequate level of protection" which can be based either on domestic law or on international commitments the third country has entered into. Transfer in this context includes

---

60   Initiative on Privacy Standardization in Europe – Final Report, 13 February 2002, available at
        http://europa.eu.int/comm/enterprise/ict/policy/standards/ipse_finalreport.pdf.
61   Data Protection Act 1998, Legal Guidance,
        http://www.informationcommissioner.gov.uk/, pp. 40–43.
62   *Ibid.*
63   Norway, Liechtenstein and Iceland.

carrying personal data on a portable computer or a PDA to a third country or sending an e-mail with personal data to a third country. When it comes to the question of uploading personal data to a web server, the European Court of Justice recently declared that uploading of personal data to a web server located in one of the EU or EEA Member States is not to be considered transfer to third country.[64] This decision actually leaves us with an unclear situation as regards to what is to be, more precisely, understood as a third country transfer.

The European Commission can adopt decisions, based on Article 25 (6) of the Data Protection Directive, declaring an adequate level of protection of a third country. At the moment, such decisions have been issued concerning Switzerland, Canada, Argentina, Guernsey and Isle of Man. When it comes to the United States, the Commission considers the US Department of Commerce's Safe Harbor Privacy Principles[65] and the transfer of Air Passenger Name Record to the United States' Bureau of Customs and Border Protection as providing adequate protection.[66] The Safe Harbor Scheme is a voluntary system of self-certification for US companies, which was implemented by the U.S. Department of Commerce. U.S. companies that self-certify and affirm that they adhere to the Safe Harbor principles, which are comparable to the data protection principles listed here, can be considered to have "an adequate level of protection" and therefore personal data may be transferred to these companies.[67]

According to Article 26 personal data may also be transferred to a third country that *does not have* an adequate level is still allowed, if:

a) "the data subject has given his consent unambiguously to the proposed transfer; or
b) the transfer is necessary for the performance of a contract between the data subject and the controller [...]; or

---

64 Judgment of the European Court of Justice of 6 November 2003, Criminal proceedings against Bodil Lindqvist., Case C-101/01.
65 2000/520/EC: Commission Decision of 26 July 2000 pursuant to Directive 95/46/EC of the European Parliament and of the Council on the adequacy of the protection provided by the safe harbour privacy principles and related frequently asked questions issued by the US Department of Commerce.
66 http://europa.eu.int/comm/internal_market/privacy/adequacy_en.htm.
67 Chissick, Michael & Kelman, Alistair, *Electronic Commerce: Law and Practice*, pp. 219.

c) the transfer is necessary for the conclusion or performance of a contract concluded in the interest of the data subject between the controller and a third party; or

d) the transfer is necessary or legally required on important public interest grounds, or for the establishment, exercise or defence of legal claims; or

e) the transfer is necessary in order to protect the vital interests of the data subject; or

f) the transfer is made from a register which according to laws or regulations is intended to provide information to the public and which is open to consultation either by the public in general or by any person who can demonstrate legitimate interest, to the extent that the conditions laid down in law for consultation are fulfilled in the particular case."

In most cases entities should ensure the consent of the data subject in order to comply with data protection legislation. This can be done either by click-wrap or e-mail and the company should state that the personal data is transferred to a third country to fulfil the requirement of informed and specific consent. For online businesses the exceptions in b and c can be applicable as well. Transfer of personal credit card information between a banking institute or the credit card company and the seller falls under c.[68]

At this point, it is worth emphasising the importance of meeting the fundamental requirements for making processing of personal data legitimate in the context of third-country transfer. As previously mentioned, it is rather unclear, following the last decision of the European Court of Justice, which technical solution (uploading, downloading, geographical location of the web server) falls under the specific rules of third-country transfer. Therefore it is even more important to ensure that the basic principles and requirements are adhered to and fulfilled.

---

68   Kuner, Christopher, *European Data Privacy Law and Online Business,* p. 218.

2.1.6.8   Rights of the data subject

The individual has the right to request from the controller information about the type and amount of personal data processed about him or her.[69] This right can also include rectification or erasure of the personal data. Differences might occur in different legal systems depending on if the data subject has an active right to request the data or if the data controller is obliged to inform the individual about any processing.

A data subject also has the right to object to any processing.[70] This means, on the one hand, that the individual can withdraw his or her previously given consent, but also in the cases of Article 7 (e) and (f) that the data subject can prevent the processing of personal data about him or her.

In addition, individuals can opt out from any direct marketing measures. This principle has been adapted in the Directive on Electronic Communication and changed to an opt-in solution. Article 13 of the Directive concerns unsolicited communications and states in (1) that "[t]he use of automated calling systems without human intervention (automatic calling machines), facsimile machines (fax) or electronic mail for the purposes of direct marketing may only be allowed in respect of subscribers who have given their prior consent."

2.1.7   Technologies that affect privacy in particular

The choice of technology very much affects the amount of personal data being processed. The EU Commission stipulated in its First report on the implementation of the Data Protection Directive: "Technological products should be in all cases developed in compliance with the applicable data protection rules. But being in compliance is only the first step. The aim should be to have products that are not only privacy-compliant and privacy-friendly but if possible also privacy-enhancing."[71]

---

69   Article 12 Data Protection Directive.
70   Article 14 Data Protection Directive.
71   COM (2003) 265(01) First report on the implementation of the Data Protection Directive (95/46/EC).

The privacy risks concerning the Internet range from browser's chattering, i.e. additional data transmitted by certain browsers in the HTTP header while making an HTTP request, as e.g. the referring page, other software installed, language, to cookies revealing the country where the user lives, his or her ISP, the typology of websites visited.[72]

The W3C already mentioned the privacy risks in the definition of the HTTP 1.1 protocol:

> "HTTP clients are often privy to large amounts of personal information (e.g. the user's name, location, mail address, passwords, encryption keys, etc.), and SHOULD be very careful to prevent unintentional leakage of this information via the HTTP protocol to other sources. We very strongly recommend that a convenient interface be provided for the user to control dissemination of such information, and that designers and implementers be particularly careful in this area. History shows that errors in this area are often both serious security and/ or privacy problems, and often generate highly adverse publicity for the implementer's company."[73]

The so-called privacy enhancing technologies (PETS) are one attempt to increase privacy protection. This term covers a wide range of applications which can include one or more of four different purposes. The four possible functions of PETS are anonymity (anonymous communication on the Internet), policy (tools that facilitate the understanding of privacy policies on websites), encryption and filtering (of cookies or for child protection).[74]

Designing a technical solution, especially in the context of e-business, affects privacy to a large extent. The more users become aware of the risks involved, the more they will choose service providers that adhere to certain technical and legal standards, either based on legislative tools or "soft law" agreements within certain industries. In addition, users will more and more utilise PETS in order to ensure their integrity.

---

72 Article 29 – Data Protection Working Party, Working document "Privacy on the Internet" – An integrated EU Approach to On-line Data Protection, Adopted 21st November 2000, pp. 14–16.
73 W3C, Network Working Group, Request for Comments: 2068, http://www.w3.org/Protocols/rfc2068/rfc2068, p. 143.
74 http://www11.informatik.tu-muenchen.de/proj/imc/pace/privacy.html.

2.1.8 Checklist for processing of personal data

The following list can serve as a checklist for making sure that the basic legal requirements are fulfilled when personal data is being processed. The different points are couched in fairly general terms and are therefore applicable to several legal systems. It has to be observed, though, that compliance with the national legislation of the establishment of the controller always has to be ensured. The following points represent some basic questions that have to be answered when personal data is being processed.

1 Is the data in question considered to be personal data?
2 Is the data being processed?
3 To what extent is the data collected for specific and legitimate purpose?
4 Is the processing fair and lawfully, i.e.
   a) did the data subject consent to the processing,
   b) is the processing necessary for the performance of a contract or the exercise of official authority?
5 Is the security of the processing ensured?
6 Is the personal data accurate and not kept longer than necessary?
7 Is the personal data transferred to a third country?
8 Are there any exceptions (depending on national legislation) applicable?

As previously mentioned, both private and public entities who process personal data have to adhere to the data protection principles. In the case of public authorities the situation is, however, somewhat different to the extent that various legal systems grant a right to access public documents. The official documents in many cases contain personal data, which gives rise to the question whether the freedom of information should prevail over the right to privacy. This is no easy question to answer, and outcomes vary depending on the country and the specific situation. The amount of personal data being processed by public authorities should not be underestimated, which is why the balance between privacy protection versus freedom of information is of the utmost importance.

2.2   Freedom of information

The expression *freedom of information* can sometimes be understood as comprising two different, but related concepts: access to information on the one hand, and freedom of expression on the other. Both principles grant rights to citizens, sometimes even including commercial enterprises, though one concerns more the receiving of information, whereas the other focuses on the spreading of information. Freedom of information as well as freedom of expression can be considered fundamental human rights.

2.2.1   Access to information

Access to information held by governments and other national authorities is important in the light of democracy and the rule of law.[75] The right of access enables public knowledge and discussion and provides a safeguard against mismanagement and corruption. In addition, the terms *openness* and *transparency* have tended to become keywords in modern governments, not the least in international organisations such as the European Union.

The main idea of access to information is that the citizens have the possibility to find out how administrations are working and if any irregularities take place in the course of public authority. In the year 2004 more than fifty countries worldwide had adopted legislation on freedom of information and in more than thirty countries Freedom of Information Acts were pending.[76]

Reasons for the increasing awareness of the right of access to information can be the growth of international pressure, especially from international organisations such as the Council of Europe,[77] the effects of the information society as more and more information in general is available to the public, anti-corruption campaigns, political changes in several countries and the recognition of freedom of information as a human right.[78]

75   Concerning the rule of law, *see* Chapter 1 in this volume, Magnusson Sjöberg, Cecilia, *Introduction to law in a digital environment.*
76   The Freedominfo.org Global Survey, Freedom of Information and Access to Government Records around the World, http://www.freedominfo.org/survey/global_survey2004.pdf.
77   See e.g. Recommendation No R (2002) 2 on access to official documents.
78   Ibid.

2.2.1.1 Basic concepts of freedom of information laws

Freedom of information as a right has been very much a national concern and is therefore mainly regulated in national legislation. Several international organisations, however, such as the European Union, stipulate access rights in their founding treaties as well.

> Article 255 of the Treaty establishing the European Community
>
> 1 Any citizen of the Union, and any natural or legal person residing or having its registered office in a Member State, shall have a right of access to European Parliament, Council and Commission documents, subject to the principles and the conditions to be defined in accordance with paragraphs 2 and 3.
>
> 2 General principles and limits on grounds of public or private interest governing this right of access to documents shall be determined by the Council, acting in accordance with the procedure referred to in Article 251 within two years of the entry into force of the Treaty of Amsterdam.
>
> 3 Each institution referred to above shall elaborate in its own rules of procedure specific provisions regarding access to its documents.

One of the first national laws on freedom of information was the Swedish Freedom of the Press Act[79], originally passed in 1766. Section 1 of today's Act stipulates that "[e]very Swedish citizen[80] shall be entitled to have free access to official documents, in order to encourage the free exchange of opinion and the availability of comprehensive information."

There are basically two different types of legal systems. On the one hand, legislation can declare all documents public unless they are to be considered secret, i.e. fulfil certain requirements (e.g. national security, law enforcement, etc.). On the other hand, the main principle can be that all documents are to be considered secret, unless they are asserted to be public.

The basic principle of the majority of freedom of information Acts is the right to access documents held by public authorities and other government bodies. The term document originally referred to paper-based documents. Due to the implementation of information

---

79 Tryckfrihetsförordningen (1949:105), http://www.riksdagen.se/english/work/fundamental/press.asp (in English).
80 In practice this right may also be taken advantage of by foreign citizens residing in Sweden, though it is not constitutionally granted.

and communication technology within public administrations,[81] digital records have also been included in the right of access.

Differences can exist in how the access is granted. In Sweden, for example, the citizen has the right either to read the material at the authority or to receive paper copies of the requested material (on payment of a fee). A right to receive public documents in electronic format does not exist at the present stage.[82] Another question in this context is whether public authorities are obliged to publish certain information, either on their website or in paper-based form.

The term *authority* can include different types of state agencies, as well as the courts, but also local and regional bodies. Private companies that are owned by the state or municipalities can be exempted.[83]

2.2.1.2 Exemptions from the right of access to information

The access right is usually not absolute, which means that in some cases other interests might be of more importance. Reasons for exemptions include national security, personal integrity and law enforcement.

The Swedish Freedom of the Press Act, for example, allows exemptions in the following cases:

> Art. 2. The right of access to official documents may be restricted only if restriction is necessary having regard to
>
> 1 the security of the Realm or its relations with another state or an international organisation;
> 2 the central fiscal, monetary or currency policy of the Realm;
> 3 the inspection, control or other supervisory activities of a public authority;
> 4 the interest of preventing or prosecuting crime;

---

81 *See also* Chapter 3 in this volume: Magnusson Sjöberg, Cecilia, *E-government.*
82 Art. 12 Freedom of the Press Act: "An official document to which the public has access shall be made available on request forthwith, or as soon as possible, at the place where it is held, and free of charge, to any person wishing to examine it, in such form that it can be read, listened to, or otherwise comprehended. Art. 13: "A person who wishes to examine an official document is also entitled to obtain a transcript or copy of the document, or such part thereof as may be released, in return for a fixed fee. A public authority is however under no obligation to release material recorded for automatic data processing in any form other than a printout except insofar as follows from an act of law.
83 This is, for example, the case in Sweden.

5 the economic interest of the public institutions;

6 the protection of the personal or economic circumstances of private subjects;

7 the preservation of animal or plant species.

Any restriction of the right of access to official documents shall be scrupulously specified in a provision of a special act of law, or, if this is deemed more appropriate in a particular case, in another act of law to which the special act refers. With authority in such a provision, the Government may however issue more detailed provisions for its application in a statutory instrument.

As the Swedish legal system is characterised by the principle of openness, the exception are regulated in detail in a "special act of law", the Secrecy Act. This statute lays down the rules for when a public document is not to be made available to a person requesting it. In some cases the whole document might be secret, in other cases only parts of the document are secret and the rest has to be handed out.

On the other hand, legal systems that support the principle of secrecy will state very specifically the conditions for a document to be available to the public. In both cases, however, the authority has to assess in the specific case following the underlying legislation whether a certain document is public or secret.

2.2.1.3 The impact of technology on freedom of information

Technology has had an immense impact on the amount of data available both to the authority itself and to the citizens accessing it. In the paper-based world documents had to be stored in archives and accessing them took time and a structured filing system of the archive.[84] Information was *frozen* at that time in decisions, letters, diaries, protocols, reports, etc. In the digital age, information is fluid and technology enables the linking together of documents, the creation of "new" documents consisting of several records from different databases and fast and easy access to a large amount of data.

---

84 Seipel, Peter, *Access Laws in a Flux*, in Seipel, Peter (ed.), *Law and Information Technology. Swedish Views – An anthology produced by the IT Law Observatory of the Swedish ICT Commission*, Swedish Government Official Reports SOU 2002:112, pp. 93–95.

In the scenario outlined, a public authority would have access to almost any data ever processed and stored in its system (or, in a networked environment, theoretically by any other public authority as well). This leads to the question of whether there should be a limit to the amount of data an authority is obliged to make available. Depending on the legal system, public administrations may only have to hand out *fixed* (either electronic or paper-based) public documents or might also be required to collect records from different databases and present them in a final *potential* document.[85] One can imagine that there is, theoretically, no technical limit to how many records can be put together. Here legislation has to decide the level of effort that the public authority must exert in order to ensure the proper balance between its own interests and the right to freedom of information.[86]

Another issue connected with the expansion of the right of freedom of information is access to software that public administrations are using. If all data held by a public authority should be included in the right to access, it is hard to distinguish between the data as such and programmes running on the authority's computer system. This also leads to the question of whether citizens should be able to test the functionality of the programs, i.e. if the authority should operate a computer program with input data supplied by the citizen. In Sweden there is no such right. The right to access, however, includes the source code of computer programs in written form.[87]

Due to the Internet, public administrations are publishing more and more information on their websites. This also impacts on the right to freedom of information. If it is possible for an authority to be excused from handing out a public document to a person requesting it simply because the document is already publicly available on a web page, the right of access is in practice unavailable to people who have no access to the Internet or are not familiar with computers or a web browser. A public authority publishing docu-

---

85 Potential documents is the term used in Swedish legislation. *See* Seipel, Peter, *Access Laws in a Flux*, p. 96.
86 In Sweden the limitation is that *potential* documents must not require more than routine measures on the part of the public authority in order to be made available. *See* Seipel, Peter, *Access Laws in a Flux*, p. 96.
87 Seipel, Peter, *Access Laws in a Flux*, p. 97.

ments on its website should at least provide the technical means for citizens to access the public information by themselves, perhaps even with help from a civil servant. Otherwise the speed of technological development increases freedom of information for some, but makes it impossible for others.

2.2.2 Freedom of information vs. privacy

As already mentioned, the right to access public information can be limited under certain conditions. This is, for example the case when personal data is concerned. Under these circumstances access to public documents is not absolute, but has to be balanced against the right to privacy.

There is no simple recipe for deciding if somebody can access a public document that contains personal data. National legislations have regulated these issues in certain laws, statues and regulations that stipulate under which circumstances which type of information can be accessed.[88] This is very often the case with certain registries, such as criminal records, DNA registries and so forth.

In other situations, the question of access has to be answered on a case-to-case basis, following the guidelines laid down in the regular data protection laws. In some legislation there might not be a conflict at all.[89] In others the public authority has to decide in each case whether or not a public document is to be considered secret or open.[90]

As a general principle the interest of the data subject may serve as a starting point. To what extent is the personal integrity of a specific person at risk if a certain public document containing data about

---

88 For a short list of special data protection laws in the Swedish public sector *see* Öman, Sören, *Implementing Data Protection in Law*, in Wahlgren, Peter (ed.), *IT-Law*, Scandinavian Studies in Law, Volume 47, Stockholm Institute for Scandinavian Law, Stockholm, 2004, pp. 399–403.

89 E.g. in the UK the Data Protection Act 1998 and the Freedom of Information Act 2000 complement each other; Macdonald QC, John, Jones, Clive H., *The Law of Freedom of Information*, Oxford University Press, New York, 2003, pp. 351–353.

90 E.g. the Swedish Secrecy Act regulates in Chapter 7, Section 16 the relation between freedom of information and privacy protection: "Secrecy applies to personal data if the access to the document would result in a processing not in accordance with the Personal Data Act." [translation by the author]. *See also* Warnling-Nerep, Wiweka, *En orientering I Tryckfrihet & Yttrandefrihet*, Stockholm, 2003, pp. 158–162.

that person is handed out? Does it matter how the document is handed out, e.g. paper-based format or electronic form? Is it of importance who requests a certain public document containing personal data? In this case, should it be possible for the public administration to verify the identity of the person requesting the document? Is it technically possible for the authority to depersonalise the document?

Problems might also arise when authorities publish official documents on their websites, e.g. decisions, minutes of meetings, reports and so forth. In some cases these documents can contain personal data and therefore be considered partly or completely secret. One also has to differentiate between minutes being handed out in written form to a single party requesting this specific document, as this might be less intrusive, and the same minutes being published on the web, where theoretically millions of people can use the data electronically.

More and more businesses are utilising personal data retrieved within the right to freedom of information from public agencies. Some legal systems might allow this under specific circumstances; other legislations might not have any restrictions at all. In Sweden personal data about citizens is gathered in the so-called "SPAR register". A specific statute regulates the use of and access to this database. Citizens can object to any use of their personal data for marketing purposes by contacting the register's administrator. [91]

2.2.3 Freedom of expression

Freedom of expression is another example of a fundamental human right. The idea behind this principle is that states should not limit free exchange of opinions and hinder citizens from expressing their ideas or their artistic creations. In this context information and communication technology has had a great impact on the possibilities of spreading ideas and opinions. As a result of both the global perspective and easy access to technology, anyone today can publish their ideas on a web page reaching millions of people.[92] The di-

---

[91] At the moment, the register is administered by one of Sweden's major legal information providers.
[92] Examples include chat, bloggs, newsgroups, etc.

mensions of the right to freedom of expression have therefore changed over the past decades. This has also an impact on other basic rights, such as privacy for example. Nevertheless, the right to freedom of expression is one of the foundations in democratic societies and has functioned well from its very inception.

Article 10 of the European Convention on Human Rights stipulates:

> 1 Everyone has the right to freedom of expression. This right shall include freedom to hold opinions and to receive and impart information and ideas without interference by public authority and regardless of frontiers. This article shall not prevent States from requiring the licensing of broadcasting, television or cinema enterprises.
>
> 2 The exercise of these freedoms, since it carries with it duties and responsibilities, may be subject to such formalities, conditions, restrictions or penalties as are prescribed by law and are necessary in a democratic society, in the interests of national security, territorial integrity or public safety, for the prevention of disorder or crime, for the protection of health or morals, for the protection of the reputation or rights of others, for preventing the disclosure of information received in confidence, or for maintaining the authority and impartiality of the judiciary.

The First Amendment of the U.S. Constitution states:

> Congress shall make no law [...] abridging the freedom of speech, or of the press [...]

The right to freedom of expression, however, is not absolute, which means it is subject to reasonable limits, such as those stated in Article 10 of the European Convention on Human Rights, e.g. national security, prevention of crime and protection of morals. Limitations on freedom of expression are often regulated in criminal law, such as child pornography and obscenity laws, hate speech legislation and the law of defamation, to name but a few.[93]

---

93 It is worth mentioning here that due to its character as a global network, questions of jurisdiction are of relevance in this context, e.g. in which country can the originator of the defamatory statement be sued. In addition question of law enforcement are of importance here, as web pages sometimes can be created anonymously which leaves only limited possibilities for the law enforcement agency to find the perpetrator.

To the extent that hate speech involving racism, xenophobia and anti-Semitism leads to a climate of intolerance and increase the barriers between groups from different national, racial, ethnic, religious or social backgrounds, national legislations forbid the publication of such information.[94]

Child pornography is another example where the expression of ideas is limited and punished by criminal law.[95] Defamation, as another example of a criminal act, means that somebody publishes a defamatory statement to third parties while he or she knew or should have known that this statement was false. In this case the freedom of expression is also limited.

In many legislations there are specific rules for newspaper publishers, radio and television stations.[96] In these cases limitations can also apply concerning advertising of tobacco, alcohol, commercial directed to children, etc.[97]

2.2.4 Freedom of expression vs. privacy

Article 9 of the Data Protection Directive states explicitly

> Processing of personal data and freedom of expression
> Member States shall provide for exemptions or derogations from the provisions [...] for the processing of personal data carried out solely for journalistic purposes or the purpose of artistic or literary expression only if they are necessary to reconcile the right to privacy with the rules governing freedom of expression.

---

94 One example for an international agreement is Council of Europe, Recommendation No R (97) 20 of the Committee of Ministers to Member States on "Hate Speech", adopted by the Committee of Ministers on 30. October 1997.
95 Council framework Decision 2004/68/JHA of 22 December 2003 on combating the sexual exploitation of children and child pornography, Article 9 Convention on Cybercrime – Offences related to child pornography.
96 In Sweden the Freedom of the Press Act applies to periodicals and "written matter". The Fundamental Law on Freedom of Expression applies to "transmissions of radio programmes which are directed to the general public and intended for reception using technical aids" (Article 6) and to "technical recordings which have been published" (Article 10). Both Acts establish specific rules for periodicals, radio and television programmes.
97 See e.g. The Swedish Radio and Television Act, http://www.rtvv.se/_upload/uk/download/rtvact.pdf.

As mentioned earlier, both privacy and freedom of expression are fundamental human rights. Their interaction, however, is not always easy to solve.

The Swedish Supreme Court, for example, found in 2001 that publication on the Internet, if made for "journalistic purposes", did not come under the data protection principles stated earlier.[98] In this case the defendant had published, on a website, personal data about specific persons who were working at a bank, claiming that they were responsible for the bankruptcy of his company. In this case it was of no importance that the defendant was not a journalist. The Supreme Court decided that "journalistic purposes" meant "to inform, criticise and create a debate on issues of interest to the public." The personal data published must, however, have some relevance to the debate. So processing of private details that do not add anything to this public debate cannot be considered legitimate under the Personal Data Act.[99] One consequence of this decision is that not only newspaper publishers can claim their rights to freedom of expression, but privacy protection also yields to the right of individuals to publish personal data in the course of public debate and discussion.

The situation is different in other countries, but the example clearly shows the impact that information technology and open networks have on fundamental rights. In principle, everybody can publish information on a website which is available to the whole world, TV stations publish news on their websites, radio stations transmit their programmes over the Internet and newspaper publishers create interactive websites with moving pictures and sound. All these examples indicate that the boundaries between TV, radio, newspapers and private websites are gradually disappearing, and the question arises whether traditional legislation is capable of covering these previously different phenomena in effectively and to what extent equality before the law is safeguarded.

---

98 Public Prosecutor v Ramsbro, Case number B 293-00 (12 June 2001), NJA 2001 p. 409.
99 *See also* Kuner, Christopher, *European Data Privacy Law and Online Business,* pp. 76–78.

2.3 Conclusions

Freedom of information and privacy protection can be said to be pulling in two opposite directions. They serve two separate purposes and guarantee two opposing interests. On the one hand individuals should be protected in their personal integrity; on the other hand individuals and legal entities, both private and public, should have the right to disseminate personal data. The balance that should be achieved will shift over time, depending on technological developments in both directions, with on the one hand technologies that can enhance the possibilities to distribute personal data and on the other ICT tools that protect personal data as much as possible.

Information security will probably affect privacy protection more than freedom of information, due to its core ideas of confidentiality (secrecy), integrity and accountability. To a certain extent, technical security is of the utmost importance in the context of privacy protection, as effective enforcement measures are needed in order to implement the legal framework.

Security issues, however, also occur when it comes to freedom of information. Depending on the legal system, official documents held by public authorities should be accessible to citizens. Specific documents might, however, be considered *secret* and should therefore not be made available. Where these documents are concerned, security might play an important role, as the choice of technique can influence the extent of documents accessible. If the system decides automatically, based on specific criteria, if a certain document is secret, the right to freedom of information can be either broadened or restricted.

All in all, the influence of information and communication technology on legal rights must not be underestimated. System design can either increase or decrease protection of individuals' rights, in the senses of both privacy and freedom of information. It is therefore important to integrate law at an early stage when developing technologies, in order to ensure that the legal system is reflected in its practical implementation.

3 E-government

Cecilia Magnusson Sjöberg

3.1 Introduction

Information technology has been gradually introduced into the area of public administration for the purpose of supporting personnel functions and financial management, case handling, calculations, statistics and office automation (document production, messaging, etc.). This chapter addresses e-government as a form of legal automation. More precisely, it concerns legal implications of the introduction and use of information technology into public administration. Current issues concern how to

- manage electronic identities and signatures in order to enhance (secure) communications with the citizens,
- avoid spam (junk mail) within governing administrative legal frameworks presupposing non-discriminating access to public agencies,
- develop methods for long-term archival of electronic records, etc.

The first era of public legal automation[1] began in some jurisdictions during period 1960–70. Politically responsible institutions introduced EDP (Electronic Data Processing) without major legal concern, a view that later proved to be inaccurate. The second era of public legal automation may be related to the years 1980–90, during which IT, generally speaking, was applied with growing legal awareness. The third era of public legal automation beginning with this century commonly referred to as e-government is still not fully adjusted to applicable legal frameworks, in spite of a deepened understanding of the impact IT has on legal infrastructures.[2] E-govern-

---

1 Automation in this context refers to the use of IT (in a broad perspective, including communication) mainly without human intervention.
2 As explained in the introductory chapter the notion of legal infrastructure may be interpreted as those part of a legal system that form the basis for data processing, communication and documentation facilities here in the context of administrative decision-making.

ment is a notion with broad meaning, partly denoting the kind of legal automation dealt with in this chapter, i.e. IT-supported case handling and decision-making in public administration. The expression e-government is, however, also used in order to describe such activities as (interactive) e-democracy by way of, for instance, e-petitioning and e-voting, which is outside the scope of this book.

The handling of (routine) mass cases in such areas as social insurance and taxation is often quoted as an example of the kind of administrative tasks for which IT support is vital in order to achieve a uniform and just application of law. From a practical point of view, it is often wise to take advantage of automatic data processing for the purpose of handling large quantities of information, e.g. data about millions of taxpayers. Another example of the benefits brought about by IT is when, due to politically based requirements of enhanced service to the citizens, cost efficiency by means of reorganisation; thousands of records must be made available in local case-handling offices nationwide. This cannot be achieved unless the information is digitally stored and distributed via electronic networks. In this context, IT support may offer financial advantages, more information storage space, and above all, increased accessibility to the information.

Historically, computers have been regarded as merely a tool for the rationalisation of public administration. Gradually, however, awareness of the legal implications of computerisation has grown in terms of understanding that IT applications are sometimes the source of legal problems, causing unfair administrative decisions in the sense of oversimplification, privacy infringements due to extensive personal data processing in electronic networks, etc.

3.2   The legal approach to e-government

3.2.1   Introduction

A study of e-government may be thought of as an interdisciplinary approach within the field of law and informatics. Focus is naturally placed on the legal framework outlined by national constitutional law (regulating legislative activities, access to public records, etc.) and administrative law (concerning the administrative procedure in primarily with regard to the handling of individual cases).

Apart from traditional sources of law, such as statutes, documents reflecting the history of law-making (e.g. government bills and public inquires), published cases, and the like, information of a less formal character must be taken into consideration when investigating e-government from a legal point of view. This is because legal automation to a large extent relates to decision-support systems. As a result, informal records, e.g. specifications of system design and program code, are central to an understanding of the field. In brief, the legal implications of e-government are in particular connected to the following factors:

- organisational context
  - legal framework
  - the need for decision support
  - potential user categories

- system management
  - system development approach
  - system design
    - domain representation
  - system administration

- responsibility
  - project organisation
    - roles and authorities
  - project management
    - routines
  - internal and external control

The handling of legal information is of primary interest when designing systems for e-government. It is difficult to foresee the legal consequences when a large number of legal sources (with varying status) are used in the course of system development – for instance, precedents which are linked together with other decided cases at a lower hierarchical level, locally decided instruments for the application of law, etc. There is an obvious risk of competence problems in this context. Practical experience shows that some kind of officially established guidelines for the handling of legal information during the system development process are advisable. A closely related question concerns the participants in the system development process. A model making use of the services of a system engineer whose task is to gather information through interviews with domain experts in order to reformulate that knowledge (including the unspoken, so called tacit knowledge) into programmable rules does not, for instance, fit into the legal framework of the public sector. The legal importance of system development may also be exemplified by the technical setting (in a broad sense). If the software to be supplied does not include the possibility to separate private (secret) records from public (official) ones, principles of openness may prove to be difficult to uphold. In conclusion, it may be said that in order to safeguard the rule of law it is necessary to bring about and realise legally oriented system development. In such a strategy, input by legal expertise in co-operation with technical professionals is of the utmost importance.

The introduction above serves the purpose of indicating that e-government interacts with public administrative law in a way that calls for specific legal attention. This statement may be further developed in terms of changes of legal infrastructures comprising mainly data processing, documentation, and communication. In fact the use of IT in public administration requires a holistic legal approach. More precisely, e-government has an impact on the formulation of legal rules as well as the application of law in individual cases.

In order to study e-government it is, in a somewhat broadened perspective, worthwhile to determine the boundaries of the kind of legal automation involved. To begin with, there is a difference between private legal automation and public legal automation. Private legal automation aims using IT in the private sector, e.g. advanced knowledge management in a business law firm or a private enterprise utilising information standards for business transactions (including e-contracting), messaging and security enhancement (using electronic signatures).

Public legal automation, on the other hand, can be understood in two ways. Firstly, public legal automation focuses on the legal consequences of IT-based administrative procedures. Secondly, public legal automation comprises questions concerning the ways in which IT can be applied – for information retrieval, decision support, etc. – during the handling of administrative matters. Expressed in another way, public legal automation may be looked upon as an interaction between computerisation (design, development, implementation, and administration) and law in the public sector. It shall be noted that the terms e-government and public legal automation here are used synonymously.

Public legal automation may be further divided into administrative automation and judicial automation. Judicial automation concerns the effects of IT within court administration with regard to judicial power, i.e. not as regards administration in general. Although the distinction between administrative automation and judicial automation is in some respects vague, it clarifies a study of e-government, since the law of administrative automation is not equivalent to the regulation of judicial administrative matters (oral procedure, etc.).

Administrative automation refers to those parts of public administration that are subject to provisions of national administrative procedure acts. Administrative activities carried out by national courts of administration consequently fall into this category of legal automation. With regard to governments (in the formal sense) an analogy can often be drawn with administrative law, where (depending on the character of the case) the applicable national administrative act is in practice applied in spite of not being formally binding in this respect.

A distinction must also be made between national administrative automation and local (municipal) administrative automation. This division is motivated by the fact that there are commonly specific legal rules governing local activities as opposed to central ones.

Legal automation in parliaments does not easily apply to any of the above categories of public legal automation. Parliamentary legal automation should rather be classified as a hybrid of legal automation with respect to the special rules in constitutional documents forming the basis of parliamentary work.

3.2.2 Characteristics of modern public administrations

Public sector administration naturally differs from one country to another, for historical, political, cultural and other reasons. Without even attempting to present any kind of comprehensive view, attention will be drawn to some characteristics of public administration.

At least three different models of public administration are conventionally used as a starting point for discussions about development trends and strategic considerations. These are the doctrines of a so-called (a) rule-based administration, (b) an administration governed by the people and (c) a market-driven one. Of course, the characteristics included in table 3.1 (below)[3] are not exhaustive and in practice public sector activities are influenced by more than one model. However, there are intrinsic differences that have an impact not only on routines for (individual) case handling but also on the way in which organisations within a public sector evolve, function and are evaluated.

The reason for bringing up doctrines of public administration in this discourse is that the governing model has an impact on choice of system development approaches as well as actual system design. In a market-driven model, for instance it might not be that important to technically ensure formal legal rights and duties according to administrative legislation. Priority may instead by given to applications that support service oriented aspects that of course may add value to the citizens, but still do not mirror the power of the state.

Table 3.1 Models of public administration.

	Rule-based	**Governed by the people**	**Market driven**
1 Perception of the state:	Compulsory institution	The tool of democracy	Service producer
2 Norm basis:	The legal	People's will	The market
3 Criterion:	The rule of law	Representation	Efficiency
4 Citizen's role:	Subject	Principal	Client
5 Relation to the surrounding society:	Independent	Politically obedient	Depending on demand
6 Model:	Court of justice	National	Private enterprise

3 The schema presented has been transformed into English from Tre förvaltningsdoktriner: några karaktäristiska drag Söderlind, Bo and Petersson, Olof, *Svensk förvaltningspolitik*, Diskurs, Uppsala, 1988, p. 30.

There is actually reason to further illustrate why the market-driven model should not be accepted without in-depth reflection. There is an important distinction to be made between a conceptual model for public administration taking the viewpoint of a customer on the market as its starting point, as opposed to a party involved in a legal process. More precisely, it is typical of the customer role that you are entitled to choose another supplier on the market if you are not happy with the service or product. Obviously this is not feasible in the context of public administration, as someone not pleased with the decision by a public agency cannot shop around for another, more favourable public official.[4]

This presentation of e-government adheres to the view that the rule of law in a service-oriented public administration is worth striving for. This implies a public administration governed by legal rules, the exercise of public authority and the major role of citizens conceived of as parties with both rights and duties. Critical factors for accomplishing public administration in compliance with the rule of law may be expressed in terms of forseeability, uniformity and openness. At the same time, efficiency ought to be an important evaluation factor. In practice, this state of affairs may be reached by making predominant principles well known to public officials as well as to the general public. A next step is to manifest the rule of law principle in legal rules and codes of procedures. In the end, goal fulfilment will of course depend on how people communicate with each other.

Considering the theme of this chapter, the following question needs to be addressed; how does e-government fit into the above-presented schema of models for public administration? The following is a tentative effort to extract certain aspects of relevance for a model focusing on e-government:

---

4   To some extent, though, rights of complaint provide a possibility of reassessment.

Table 3.2 A model of e-government.

	E-governed
1 Perception of the state:	Welfare provider
2 Norm basis:	Information society
3 Criterion:	Trust
4 Citizen's role:	Contracted party
5 Relation to the surrounding society:	Technology sensitive and based on networking
6 Model:	E-business (not necessarily e-commerce though)
7 Professional role:	Application designer

The perception of the state is that of a welfare provider, which could also be referred to as the performing state. The norm basis is that of the modern information society in which information and communications technology play an important role. The criterion for evaluation and development is trust among the citizens. Trust is a concept that in its legal sense resembles the kind of values captured by the notion of the rule of law. However, the trust concept is more vague and subjective in its character.[5] The relation to the surrounding society is technology-sensitive and based on networking. E-business in the broad sense is the predominant model, being inspired both by e-commerce activities and conventional public sector tasks. A typical professional role in e-government activities is that of an application designer or in a broader perspective an information architect. This implies the need for crossover competence beyond that of conventional legal and technical ones.

3.2.3 Public sector infrastructures

There is no doubt that e-government brings about changes in public sector (legal) infrastructures. One characteristic feature of an infrastructure is the difficulty of predicting its effect. In other words, the

---

5 In fact it might prove meaningful to try to develop a more precise meaning in terms of well-founded as well as unfounded trust and mistrust (from a legal point of view).

consequences of infrastructural changes in the legal domain are usually difficult to define beforehand. System development methods may serve as an example of a process which may seem to be of a purely technical and administrative nature, with no particular legal implications. An in-depth analysis reveals, however, that the design of legal decision support systems comprises a number of complicated legal issues with regard to the handling of legal information, etc. The reason is, of course, that during system development procedures it is necessary to make specific decisions concerning organisational matters, ways of data processing and documentation – all of which changes the foundations of rule formulation, rule application and the transparency of public administration.

3.2.3.1 Networking organisations

The large-scale information systems used by public authorities exchanging an enormous amount of data constitute the underlying structure of public administration. Well-established as well as emerging networks of computer-based systems have changed the possibilities for the control of public information flows. Experience shows that a considerable number of public (administrative) information systems have turned out to be so complicated with regard to system architecture and their functions that public authorities have partly lost control over them, due to inconsistent procedures in computer programs, insufficient data quality, etc.

The merger of the public and the private sectors is another sign of infrastructural changes. In this context the use of IT emphasises the general tendency in society. One consequence of this is that the application of law takes place in a setting where public tasks are mixed with private undertakings. This happens, for instance, when public authorities outsource functions that were previously taken care of internally. When private enterprises are practically in charge of running e-government applications there is a risk of the foundations of legislation being severely affected. Moreover, insight into public affairs may become more restricted from the citizen's point of view because of such privatisation of public engagements.

Another sign of infrastructural changes is the growing dependence of administrative procedures on the support of consultants. The engagement of private enterprises, however, is nothing exceptional in the management of e-government. For instance, public authorities responsible for environmental protection have long been hiring consultants to carry out measurements and analyses of polluted lakes or watercourses. Commissionable work usually concerns the control of one particular company in order to examine whether or not the conditions for the permit to carry out so-called "contaminating" activities are complied with. When, on the other hand, consultants are hired to program national public information systems, their participation in and influence on the administrative procedure are of quite another dimension, since such a system development project may in some aspects correspond to legislative activities. The reason for this statement is based on the fact that the outcome of individual cases is in practice based on the design and the implementation of the information system.

The development towards networking organisations is further realised by means of data exchange between administrations and private enterprises. When public authorities acquire on-line access to private information systems in order to obtain credit information, bibliographical data, etc., enforcement of privacy and secrecy protection legislation is affected. To further exemplify, data which can be reached via a public information system may in some jurisdictions be regarded as in the keeping of an agency and thus to be made public to the general public on request. Adding to the picture, there are car salesmen with external access to national motor vehicle registers, and real estate agents having connections to national real estate systems. Although only public information (official documents/records) is to be made externally accessible, there is always a risk of unauthorised access to (secret documents) and distortion of data, which is associated with telecommunications.

3.2.3.2 Automatic data processing

The expression "data processing" refers here to automatic methods of case handling. It comprises such activities as word processing, information retrieval, calculations, data comparisons, data interchange, etc. With regard to the administrative procedure, one important feature related to the use of information technology is speed. Computerisation has made it possible for public officials to make legal decisions in a comparatively short period of time. The rule of law, however, requires not only rapid case handling but also sufficiently high quality of data management. In an evaluation of automatic case handling it is therefore necessary to consider not only the gain in time but also the amount of faulty decisions to be expected due to incorrect or misleading data processing.

Legal automation in public administration is often described in terms of large-scale and complex information systems. Another characteristic of automation is independence of (geographical) distance. On the other hand this facilitates the handling of legal information, but it also carries a risk of privacy infringements as a result of excessive data collection.

When it comes to the essence of automatic data processing, the following points need to be considered in particular. Computerisation of public administration presupposes a varying degree of preparatory clarifications concerning the specific implementation of administrative procedures. When a specific interpretation of a legal rule or a decided case has been implemented into the system it will – in practice, though not formally gain the quality of precedent for all forthcoming cases.

3.2.3.3 Electronic documentation

Administrative law is characterised by legal principles and rules that have been drawn up to suit manual, individual case handling. In contrast, many information systems in public administration have been designed for automatic, mass administration of cases. In addition to this, the legal framework of public administration has been designed for a paper-based process and not paper-less case handling. Among other things, the introduction of IT means that traditional administrative law has to be adjusted to the new conditions of electronic record keeping, as well as procedures for electronic identification and signing.

Case handling in a digital environment is more dynamic – changeable – compared with traditional administrative procedures. This is because dynamic documents are intrinsically different from static administrative paper files. Although IT may support the administrative procedure, there are risks associated with its comprehensive copying and editing possibilities. This is one underlying legal reason for obligations to file electronic records.

3.3 Major problem areas

In this chapter the wide range of problem areas related to e-government is narrowed down to the following three: (a) IT-related rule formulation, (b) IT-related rule application, and (c) openness and access to public documents.

3.3.1 IT-related rule formulation

The problem area referred to as IT-related rule formulation comprises three different aspects of legal automation, namely: rule transformation, formalised supervision and distribution of competence.

The development of information systems for the purpose of decision-making often means that vague criteria characterising natural legal language must be transformed into more precise (strict) criteria in the sense of programmable data. This is because most computer programs need clear operational facts in order to be executed.

Both theoretical and empirical studies show that the transformation of legal rules into program code is not a trivial task from the legal point of view. In several fields, e.g. social insurance and security, and study loan administration, misinterpretations of statutes have occurred in the corresponding computer programs. Another problem is that faulty programming methods may lead to ambiguous results even if the outcome of the automatic data processing is not entirely wrong. An important point to make in this context (see also above) is that the initial rule transformation will determine the outcome of almost all the following cases, since in practice the implemented interpretation of legal rule(s) is made once and for all. Consequently, the value of the right to appeal an individual administrative decision may be questioned when the real decision-making lies in the design of the information system.

In principle, the transformation from legislation to instructions in program code may be discussed in terms of:

a) an administrative action of no particular (legal) interest,
b) a singular interpretation and application of legal rules (i.e. individual decision making),

c) the issuing of new rules (i.e. general administrative decision making), or

d) as a special kind of administrative decision-making.

Sometimes legal rules are programmed without any alterations during the system development procedure. At other times rules expressed in a computer program may turn out to be quite different as compared to the corresponding legislation. It can then be argued that the transformation should be rather looked upon as the issuing of new (legal) rules. In such a situation a number of questions arise, e.g. to what extent the computer program complies with the fundamental laws of the national jurisdiction in question.

3.3.1.1   Formalised supervision

The tradition of law making has been changing over a long period of time. In contrast to earlier casuistic legislation a tendency towards more generally formulated provisions may be noted. Yet another regulatory development is that of technically neutral legislation in response to the rapidly increased use of IT-applications for data processing, dissemination, archival, etc.

Usually, provisions formulated in general terms are supplemented by provisions at a lower level of the norm hierarchy (decrees issued by government and/or regulations issued by a central public agency), by case law and in some cases even by contracts. In the context of e-government, computer programs have come to function as a fourth category of supplement with the purpose of formalisation of supervision activities.

There are in fact branches of public administration that are, so to speak, programmed but not constitutionally regulated. Over the years examples of this phenomenon may, for instance, be found in the area of environmental protection. In this field of public administration, computer programs calculating the values of permitted emissions (according to a decision made by an authority) and comparing them with reported emissions constitute a kind of formalised supervision, although neither the requisites for data input nor the algorithms are explicitly expressed in any specific legal regulation.

3.3.1.2 Distribution of competence

In spite of the fact that local agencies conventionally are formally in charge of the handling of individual cases, the outcome of an administrative matter is in reality often determined in centrally designed information systems, where taxes are calculated, registers linked together, etc. The local responsibility is thereby reduced to the input of data forming the basis of central data processing.

If, for instance, a piece of program code differs so much in comparison with the corresponding conventional legal rule(s) that the computer program qualifies (because of its similarities to a conventional legal rule in the sense of being general and binding) as an act of legislation, it must fit into the formal (national) structure of law-making.

To conclude, it is essential to analyse the transformation process in order to establish whether a new legal rule is at hand or whether it is an expression of an already existing (legal) rule. In the situation when new legal rules are expressed in the form of computer program it must be possible to deduce authority from governing constitutional documents, and also to make the IT-related rule formulation conform to the principles of how provisions are to be enacted.

3.3.1.3 Authorisation of program code

There are several reasons why it is essential that public authorities authorise (some of) their computer programs. Depending on the severity of the interpretation of the statutes serving as a basis for the design of the corresponding program(s), the procedure of system development ought to be controlled. It is, for instance, important to establish the formal authority (competence) of the participants – public officials and consultants, technicians, user representatives et al. – in order to transform legal rules and decided cases into transactions in program code.

The legal status of a computer program is obviously not only relevant with regard to activities taking place during actual system development procedure but also when a system is in use. It is furthermore important to consider the legal status of program code in the situations of correction and reconsideration of decisions, as well as with regard to complaints. Another reason why it is important to determine the legal status of computer programs in public administration is that legal rules expressed in the program code might need authorisation in accordance with a nation's fundamental laws.

Consequently, authorisation of program code in public administrations serves the purpose of creating legally well-organised, orderly conditions for IT-related formulation. In this way, the rule of law can be safeguarded.

3.3.2   IT-related rule application

IT-related rule application has become a common feature of public administration, and as a matter of fact the normal way of case handling in the 21st century. To give a few examples, mention can be made of civil servants in a social insurance organisation who register data on computer files; decisions about different kinds of social benefits are then made automatically. One may also refer to information systems for customs formalities, which commonly include routines for automatic decision-making. Also the design of taxation systems is often based on the principles of automatic administrative procedure, etc.

Although legal automation is no longer anything unusual, the kind of IT support utilised in different cases varies a lot. Sometimes the administrative procedure is almost completely automated. This is the case when the collection of and the processing of data, as well as notification of decisions, is done exclusively with the aid of IT. The technological support for the administrative procedure may also be only partial, e.g. with regard to certain printing routines. IT-related rule application thus includes both automatically made decisions as well as decision-making where IT plays only a peripheral role.

One of the key issues in e-government is the interaction between IT-related rule application and underlying administrative procedure acts. Generally speaking, administrative legislation is formally applicable to legal automation in the sense of automatic case handling (to a full extent or only partly). This is not always made explicit, however, in a legal instrument but sometimes only in a statement contained in preparatory works. Furthermore, the degree to which the provisions of this kind of administrative legislation have been IT-adjusted varies a lot.

From a citizen's point of view, e-government presents both advantages and disadvantages. There are, for instance, possibilities of strengthening the rule of law with regard to rules concerning service duties of agencies and the co-operation between agencies. One reason for this is that the use of IT facilitates the exchange of data between agencies as well as with the general public.

On the other hand, empirical studies of legal automation in combination with what comes out of decided cases have shown that the fundamental legal principles concerning, e.g., the openness of the administrative procedure may be threatened by the increase of e-government. In an IT environment it is, for example, not obvious how to interpret and apply rules governing the following kind of actions:

- submission,
- recording of information,
- the right of parties to be informed,
- stating reasons for decisions
- notification of decisions,
- the right to complain, and
- how to complain about a decision.

Furthermore, the use of IT calls for specific legal attention when it comes to the application of rules concerning:

- filing of (electronic) documents,
- correction of errors, and
- reconsideration of decisions.

One reason for this is that incorrect data processing may be caused by the associated computer program if producing erroneous administrative decisions in all the cases decided automatically. At the same time other kinds of mistakes occurring in data processing, due, for instance, to mistakes committed when entering the data, may not depend on any corresponding computer program and will therefore cause fewer incorrect administrative decisions.

There is one category of administrative rules which present no particular problems. Although regulations of, for instance, oral handling and voting often are formally applicable to automatic case handling, legal automation has so far caused no particular problems. More advanced forms of e-government may in the future, however, bring about uncertainties in connection with the development and the use of electronic case handling systems, regarding e.g. different kinds of on-line data transmission.

3.3.3   Openness and access to public documents

The third of the main problem areas dealt with in this chapter concerns transparency of e-government.[6] There are in fact three kinds of openness which are of particular relevance in a discussion about e-government. To begin with, mention should be made of principles of publicity commonly stipulated in freedom of information legislation. Secondly, privacy protection legislation typically regulates a right of data subjects to receive information about personal data processing concerning him or her. Thirdly, the right of parties to be informed according to general administrative regulations is usually applicable in an IT environment.

The problem area of openness and access to public documents contains a number of key issues. One important problem with political implications concerns the character of IT-adjusted rights of access. In fact e-government may both strengthen and weaken the applicability of principles of publicity. The conflicts of interests encountered here concern the rights to publicity and the need for secrecy as well as the right to privacy as opposed to efficiency.

The development of a legal terminology for the purpose of creating a legal framework for the handling of electronic records has proved to be another key issue. Decisions concerning legal interpretations of expressions such as "accessibility" and "routine measures" seem to create a lot of problems in an IT environment.

Further, the basis for secrecy classifications has changed, due to the computerisation of public administration. Traditionally the responsible public official would decide on matters concerning secrecy, following a direct request to disclose some specific piece of information. There has been a tendency, however, to work out – and technically implement – general rules regarding decisions about secrecy beforehand, to facilitate decisions as to whether a certain kind

---

6   Freedom of information and expression as well as privacy protection in general
    was dealt with in the previous Chapter 2, authored by Christine Kirchberger.

of information should be subject to secrecy. The presently widespread electronic information exchange between public authorities has in fact become a major challenge to the application of secrecy legislation in an IT environment. Consequently, close attention should be paid to the principle of publicity, as well as other legal regulations, already at the stage of designing information systems.

3.4 Concluding remarks

Network organisations, automatic data processing and electronic documentation, etc. give rise to a great variety of legal questions which are not always easy to grasp and structure. The basis for this chapter has been traditional public (administrative) law. This means that legal implications of infrastructural changes have been discussed in terms of IT-related rule transformation (including formalised supervisory activities, distribution of competence), IT-related rule application and transparency. The analysis boils down to the main conclusion that there is a need for combination of measures, for instance, authorisation of program code and legally oriented system development.

Historically the political interest in legal automation for public administration has concentrated on adjustments of principles of publicity (open government) and on the implementation of privacy legislation. Theoretical studies as well as practical experiences show, however, that the legal implications of the introduction and use of IT have a much wider range than these two problem areas would imply.

The openness of public activities and the protection of privacy are of course important legal safeguards in a society adhering to the rule of law. It may be argued, however, that an adjustment of the legal rules regulating the administrative procedure as well as the constitutional framework for the issuing of legal norms is even more urgent. In practice comparatively few people take advantage of rights of access to official public documents. On the other hand in fact every citizen is affected by automatic case handling routines in such areas as social insurance and taxations.

In a few words of conclusion, it may be said that it is not possible to reduce information and communications technology as merely a means of rationalisation comparable with other administrative tools. Instead, IT must be regarded as a powerful resource which has to be managed from the legal point of view. A combination of measures is required in order to let the traditional principles of legality prevail. Integration of law into system design, development and management will serve this purpose.

4 Intellectual property rights on the Internet

Mikael Pawlo

4.1 Copyright

The creator or author of an original, intellectual work will automatically obtain a form of protection.[1] This form of protection is called copyright. Copyright was, as well as other forms of intellectual property rights, formed "to Promote the Progress of Science and the useful Arts by securing for limited times to Authors and Inventors the exclusive right to their respective writings and discoveries," as it says in the United States Constitution.[2] The work may be literary, musical, artistic or otherwise an intellectual work of art. A book may be subject to copyright, as well a song or a play.

The form of expression does not matter. You will obtain protection if the work is fixed in a tangible form. Basically, if you can touch, hear or see the work, you may be eligible for copyright protection. The fixation of the work does not have to be directly accessed. If the work is communicated with the help of a certain device or machine it may still be copyrighted. Copyrightable works include categories as: literary works, musical works, dramatic works, sculptural works, movies and other audiovisual works, sound recordings and architectural works. Computer works are regarded as literary works in copyright law. Ideas and discoveries are not protected by copyright law. They may instead be protected by patent protection (see below).

The copyright becomes the property of the author as soon as the work is created. One prerequisite for copyright protection is that the work is original. If the work is too trivial copyright protection will not be granted. Thus, the words "hello world" are not protected by

---

1 This is a general description of copyright law, written for international technology students. Local and national variations may occur.
2 See U.S. Const. Art. I, Sec. 8, Cl. 8.

copyright, while this chapter as a whole is. One simple test to see if a work is original enough for copyright protection is to examine whether two individuals would come up with exactly the same work should they decide to write, for example, a chapter on copyright in a law textbook for techies. If the result is likely to be the same (i.e. "hello world"), then the work probably should not be protected by copyright. Copyright may only be claimed by the author or individuals or entities that have derived the rights from the original author or his licensees.

Copyright protection is commonly granted without prior registration. In Sweden, registration of copyright is not possible. In the U.S. registration is available, but not necessary in order to obtain protection. Many choose to register their works to create a public record of their creation. In the U.S. registered works are eligible for statutory damages and coverage of attorney's fees in case of a successful litigation. Some people, both in the U.S. and Sweden choose to create a so-called poor man's copyright. A poor man's copyright is a simple way of obtaining evidence of first creation, being the author of a certain work, by sending a copy of the work to oneself by certified mail. Although this may be a nice piece of evidence in a court of law or in a settlement litigation, it is no substitute for registration in the U.S.

The copyright symbol (c) is used in copyright statements, for example "This text is (c) Copyright 2005 Mark Twain". It is not necessary to obtain protection. The date used in a copyright statement has nothing to do with when the protection will expire. The copyright statement is mostly a way of showing when the work was originally created and of claiming ownership and authorship. If several years are assigned (This text is (c) Copyright 2005, 2006 Mark Twain) this means the work was amended or modified. The first date is the first date of creation, the second the date of modification.

Copyrighted works are commonly protected (with some exceptions) until at least fifty (50) years have passed since the year the author died. In many countries, such as the U.S. and the European Union Member States, the protection for most works lasts up until seventy (70) years have passed since the year the author died. This is the copyright term.

Copyright is a protection which grants the author the exclusive right to reproduce to work in the form of copies during the copyright term. It is also an exclusive right to creative derivative works, to distribute perform and display the work in public. The term exclusive in copyright means that the author alone may decide how the work is to be exploited. If someone distributes copies in other ways than the author has designated and such distribution is not within the limits of fair use or otherwise permitted by law, an infringement of the author's copyright has occurred. Such an infringement may be punished with liability and damages but also by a penal sentence for a serious offence. The author may exercise his exclusive right to reproduce the work through a licence agreement. The licence agreement is nothing more than a contract specifying how, when and where a work may be used and copied. The licence agreement is the most powerful tool in the author's toolbox. The author may charge his audience through his licence agreement, he or she may designate a publisher and he or she may even choose to not exercise the exclusive rights granted by copyright law. The author may, if they please, choose to stand back and offer their work freely for anyone. Why would an author choose to do that? One reason may be the moral rights.

Authors create works to be rewarded. However, such a reward is not only monetary. Authors also like to be recognised for their creative effort. The moral rights are an idea deriving from the French Revolution, when the concept of a "droit moral" was introduced, dealing with this issue. The concept has nothing to do with morals, but with the personal and reputational connection between an author and his work. Or as the French philosopher Bouffler puts it: "S'il existe pour un homme une veritable propriété, c'est sa pensée." In short, the moral rights are the right to integrity and the right of attribution. The right of integrity is an absolute, non-transferable right to get respect for the work as such. This means that the work shall not be displayed or used in a fashion the author does not approve of, such as a musical work used in a pornographic movie. The right to attribution is a right to be named as the author of the work. Moral rights are strong in Europe, but less so in the U.S. In the U.S. moral rights are established through interpretation of several copyright, trademark, privacy, and defamation statues. However, even in the U.S. authors of works of visual arts get moral rights protection for their works as long as they are alive.

Copyright is a national protection, which may pose a problem when works are distributed over the Internet. However, through the Berne Union for the Protection of Literary and Artistic Property (the "Berne Convention"), the signatories – comprising most Western countries – have harmonised their respective copyright laws to the extent provided in this chapter. Thus, all Western countries and other signatories to the Berne Convention will protect the works of other nationals the same way the country concerned protects the works of its nationals. Hence, the Internet will not become a lawless zone where legal havens – where copyright is disregarded – are automatically created online.

Another issue is enforcement. The courts will not look the other way in respect of copyright infringement just because the infringement took place through the Internet. But the courts may have a hard time establishing the proper jurisdiction and competent court to try the infringement. There is also the problem of technology. A lot of technological measures could be taken to make law enforcement of copyright infringement harder.

John Perry Barlow has stated in a famous essay on the future of copyright (The Economy of Ideas[3]) that:

> "In Cyberspace, there are not only no national or local boundaries to contain the scene of a crime and determine the method of its prosecution, there are no clear cultural agreements on what a crime might be. Unresolved and basic differences between European and Asian cultural assumptions about intellectual property can only be exacerbated in a region where many transactions are taking place in both hemispheres and yet, somehow, in neither."

However, Mr Barlow has not taken into account that the courts will not look the other way if a copyright infringement is committed. The courts will establish jurisdiction and find what law to apply. Hence, copyright will continue in force, even on the Internet in the digital era. Another issue is of course whether this is suitable or "good". This is further examined below ("The great debate").

When you surf the Internet with a web browser you will consume a lot of copyrighted material. You will be exposed to text, pictures, sounds and even movies. You will use a copyrighted computer pro-

---

3   Online under http://www.eff.org/~barlow/EconomyOfIdeas.html.

gram (or "software") to access the web pages. The web pages will be built of copyrighted code and databases. Such use of copyrighted content is commonly granted. You will get a free licence or a licence will be implied by the web page owner. This is just a licence to view. Just because the picture is posted on a web page, this does not mean that you obtain a licence to republish the picture on your own web page, probably not even by using a hyperlink.[4] Further, you may only download music, computer programs and pictures and make such works available insofar as it is permitted by law or a licence is granted by the copyright holder.

Several kinds of infringements take place through the Internet. One is of course the plain download of copyrighted material, such as computer programs, music and movies from a web page. Such infringements were common in the early days of the Internet. Then came peer-to-peer networks such as Napster. Peer to Peer-networks are defined as a computer network that does not have fixed clients and servers, but a number of peer nodes that function as both clients and servers to the other nodes on the network.[5] With peer-to-peer networks the copying of works became much more efficient and harder to control and infringements harder to proceed against. It is one thing to identify a web page where a copyrighted work is offered for free download. It is a completely different and more difficult thing to identify a Bittorrent stream, where the file is simultaneously downloaded from several different sources in small parts. In such cases, the file is not downloaded from one single source, but from several, and it is hard to identify the infringer(s). Technological measures will be taken to fight even Bittorrent downloads, but it is clear that the legal situation and the technical situation is becoming more and more interrelated.

All downloads and copies without license agreements do not constitute infringements. Sometimes you are allowed to copy works without the prior consent of the copyright holder or author. This is called the exception for fair use in the U.S. or exception for private

4   This is an internationally very much discussed legal position, but most legal scholars of 2004 argue that a hyperlink which publishes a work from another web page on your own page as if it were your own picture may constitute copyright infringement. Opinions may differ in different jurisdictions, though.
5   From Wikipedia, http://en.wikipedia.org/wiki/Peer_to_peer (as available on September 20, 2004).

use and the right to quote in EU law. Without going into detail about this highly complex set of rules one may establish certain principles. The fair use is an attempt by the legislator to balance the interest of the public and the interest of the copyright holder. This is achieved by allowing certain identified uses that would otherwise constitute infringement. One of the uses is the right to time-shift movies. This is basically a U.S. exception, based on the famous Betamax recorder case, but it applies widely in several jurisdictions. What is time-shift? It is a way to see works at other times than when they where broadcast. Or as I would put it – the right to tape a show on TV. Another exception is the right to make a parody of the work. This is a complicated issue, since the concept of parody varies from nation to nation, but in most jurisdictions a basic parody is allowed. You may also include a part of a work as a description, comment, analysis or review of the work or its effects in society (or elsewhere). Hence, copyright holders can not discourage criticism, for example, by claiming that a certain review constitutes copyright infringement.

4.2   Trademarks and domain names

Trademark protection protects words, phrases and symbols identifying the source and origin of a product or service. A trademark is protected following registration or consistent use. Trademarks shall be distinctive and consumers shall be able to see differences between different trademarks for different products. A trademark applicant files his application with his national trademark office.[6] The trademark office will grant the application following review, which may take as long as several years in some jurisdictions (including Sweden). Therefore many companies start using the trademarks even before they are registered. The risk is of course that the trademark applications will not be granted, due to non-distinctiveness. However, consistent use may also be a ground for registration, and so use of this kind is not subject to high risk. Another risk is that the trademark will be confused with another company's trademark. Then the

---

6   Or in cases of international registration to the OHIM in Alicante (European Community Trademark) or relevant federal authority.

use may infringe that company's trademark rights. To avoid such situations most companies perform trademark searches before launching a new brand name. Such searches are conducted through investigation of public records over registered trademarks, which will not catch up any trademarks which are protected by consistent use rather than registration.

A trademark may consist of any signs capable of being represented graphically, even the shape of goods or of their packaging, provided that such signs are capable of distinguishing the goods or services of one undertaking from those of other undertakings. The most common registration will probably be of words, designs, letters, personal names and numerics, but following the community trademark in the EU and harmonisation, a more liberal attitude to what is registrable now prevails than was normal in most EC countries before the new CTM and Harmonization directive[7]. Even smells, sounds and colours may be registered as trademarks, but it is a little more complicated process than registering, for example, words. However, it is used – in the U.S. the sound of a roaring lion is protected as a trademark for motion pictures. The sound of a Harley-Davidson has also been protected. A lot of colours have been protected for certain uses.

A trademark is registered for separate classes of products or services. The same word may be held by separate trademark holders for different products or services. For example, the boat engine named Solo may co-exist with the soda Solo. The basis of trademark law and trademark protection is to protect the public from being confused or deceived about the origin and quality of a product or service. Trademarks are a market tool to distinguish a certain product from other similar products on the market.

A domain name is not in legal terms a trademark, but is very similar to a word mark in its construction. A domain name is registered to identify a specific web resource and to simplify the addressing of email. There are alternative dispute resolutions in place for many top level domain name systems. This means that disputes can be settled out of court in simplified, quicker and cheaper procedures than in a court. Often – as a general rule – a trademark owner will be

---

7   First Council Directive 89/104/EEC of 21 December 1988 to approximate the laws of the Member States relating to trade marks (Harmonization Directive).

able to obtain a domain name with a similar wording as the trademark through the alternative dispute resolution. On factor complicating things is that there are no trademark classes for domain names. Hence, both Solo the boat engine and Solo the soda may have a valid claim for Solo.se, but only one may obtain the registration. The solution is a first-come-first-served approach.

The symbol (TM) is sometimes used in conjunction with a word or symbol. This means that the company using the word or symbol claims trademark protection and considers the word or symbol its trademark. The symbol (R) is sometimes also used. This means that the word or symbol has been duly registered with the relevant trademark authority. In many jurisdictions it is not permissible to use the (R) symbol, should the company not have registered its trademark, and so the (R) symbol is a rather good indicator of whether the mark is registered or not.

Trademarks may be used by competitors and consumers and journalists in order to compare products, conduct reviews and so forth. However, trademarks may not be used to create confusion over the rightful proprietor of a certain good or service. Trademarks are an important identifier to consumers and protected as such. Thus, it is not permissible to use other companies' trademarks and logotypes to create interest in products and services offered by your own company. It is still debated whether you may use other companies' trademarks in your meta-tags[8] or otherwise manipulate search engines to send other companies' customers to your website, but most legal scholars in most Western jurisdictions consider this a non-permissible action.[9]

4.3   Patents

Patents protect inventions or discoveries. Ideas and discoveries are not protected by copyright law. Patents give the holder an exclusive right to use and license use of an invention for a certain period. The exclusive right will provide the holder with the right to exclude

---

8   A part of the HTML code building a web page that is only read by search engines.
9   It may be considered unfair competition or trademark infringement.

others from making, selling, marketing, using or even importing the invention. The time of protection is typically 20 years from the filing date of a patent application with a possible prolongation for another term of protection. The patents are dealt with in similar ways to copyrighted works, through licence agreements. What is the relevance of this on the Internet? The Internet is built upon software and ideas.

Software has traditionally been protected by copyright, the same way books are. The protection for books has been around for a long time and seems to be working quite well. The protection of software is a newer phenomenon and software has little in common with books. The copies are produced and look different and so is the manufacturing of the copies. Even the creation of a book and that of software differs. One alternative to copyright protection is patents. Some argue that software should be patented instead of copyrighted.

To the advantages of software patents one could add that the developers get a stronger and more distinct protection of their works. However, the big problem with software patents is that they protect ideas and technical innovations. The big advantage of not granting software patents is that it is legal without cross-licensing to write two software programs that solve the same problem and conduct the same assignment, with no risk of copyright or patent infringement. Granting software patents, the second software program could constitute an infringement of the first software program, should the programs give the same technical effect.

It is stipulated in the Swedish Patent Act that software should never be considered an invention in the sense of the Patent Act, and so an applicant never should be granted a patent based on software. This principle derives from the European Patent Convention and was implemented in the Swedish Patent Act effective from 1st July 1978. The principle was established in practice even before that. However, in spite of the above, it is not impossible to be granted a patent for software in Sweden. In practice, the Patent Office shall make a comprehensive study of the application/innovation and the fact that a part of the application is a software program shall not as such rule out the possibility of a patent being granted. Among other things, the Patent Office will determine the technical effect of the innovation. Still, there is a difference between this judgement and the new EU writing that would endorse software patentability. The question is how to determine the technical effect.

Another development is patents for business methods. Such patents are not yet available in Europe, but are common in the U.S. Business methods could for example be the well-known way of shopping at Amazon.com with one single mouse click (so-called one-click-shopping).

4.4   The great debate and the way ahead

The expansion of the protection of intellectual property has spurred quite a debate. Some even contend that the term "intellectual property" is misleading. The use of the word "property" may suggest that the works should be compared to physical property, whereas in fact the ownership is a state-granted monopoly which is limited in scope and time. The key issue of this debate and the million-dollar question is: "when will the protection of current works and innovations stifle the creation of new works and innovations?"

The debate sometimes resembles a religious debate. The scientific and empirical evidence is non-evident and a lot of the arguments are based on logic rather than hard facts. This makes the debate hard to follow and it also puts the policy-makers in a tough spot. How should one legislate when current intellectual property owners want stronger protection but such an expansion may be cannibalising on the creation of future works? To this mix of confused arguments you should add peer-to-peer file sharing and the Internet, software patentability and you end up with a highly complex picture. Then there is the question of whether copyright is secured for "limited times" when works are protected for seventy years following the year the author died? When it comes to computer programs such protection is similar to perpetual protection, since computers are developed and changed such a way that computer programs become worthless within a few years of their release. The same arguments are sometimes used for literature and other works.

When it comes to software patents, researchers James Bessen and Robert M. Hunt have studied software patents from an empirical perspective and found that they are used to claim certain business areas in a way that leads to less ventures in research and development and not increased research. Deeper discussion is needed concerning the protection of software and related innovations. There is a clear and justified need for developers to get protection for their works. However, it is not evident that software patents will correspond to that need. It seems to me that software patents might instead create a situation where the development of software ceases and where patents obstruct further progress in IT and the Internet. Maybe legislators should try to find a new sui generis protection of software that is not copyright nor patents, but this is still far-fetched in practice and may – or may not – happen in the future.

One way of addressing the issue regarding copyright, if you do not like the expansion of intellectual property rights, is by offering new ways of licensing content. The copyright proprietor may, as discussed above, freely decide how and when his works should be distributed. Through the free software movement a new way of looking at the distribution, development and essentially – sharing.

Free software is a matter of the users' freedom to run, copy, distribute, study, change and improve the software.[10] More precisely, it refers to four kinds of freedom, for the users of the software:

- The freedom to run the program, for any purpose (freedom 0).
- The freedom to study how the program works, and adapt it to your needs (freedom 1). Access to the source code is a precondition for this.
- The freedom to redistribute copies so you can help your neighbour (freedom 2).
- The freedom to improve the program, and release your improvements to the public, so that the whole community benefits (freedom 3). Access to the source code is a precondition for this.

Free software is very simple in its construction. It uses the provisions of copyright law whereby the author has an exclusive economic right in his work. In copyright law, computer programs are regarded as literary works. Thus, the author of a computer program can enter into any agreement regarding his work. One such agreement is the GNU GPL. GNU GPL stands for GNU General Public License. The GNU GPL is the licence agreement that applies the four freedoms

10 See http://www.gnu.org/.

above to the licensing scheme of computer programs. The European debate on interoperability ended in 1991, when the European Union introduced a Directive on the Legal Protection of Computer Programs. That Directive excludes ideas underlying any element of a computer program, including its interfaces, from copyright protection. It also specifically permits disassembly of computer programs in order to achieve interoperability. Transparency is therefore ensured, but without access to the source code of the computer program it would still be hard to disassemble and interpret the functions of the computer programs. The GNU GPL wants to solve this by always forcing the developer to disclose and distribute his software.

The free software movement has inspired the creation of Creative Commons.[11] Creative Commons is an online resource where authors of works other than computer programs may designate their licensing terms, in similar ways to the GNU GPL. You may for example choose that your works be distributed freely in a non-commercial environment, while commercial distribution will be subject to your prior consent and possibly a fee. Creative Commons describe its efforts like this:

> "We use private rights to create public goods: creative works set free for certain uses. Like the free software and open-source movements, our ends are co-operative and community-minded, but our means are voluntary and libertarian. We work to offer creators a best-of-both-worlds way to protect their works while encouraging certain uses of them – to declare 'some rights reserved.'

> "Thus, a single goal unites Creative Commons' current and future projects: to build a layer of reasonable, flexible copyright in the face of increasingly restrictive default rules."

When this chapter was composed the EU's Infosoc Directive, also known as the European Union Copyright Directive, was being implemented throughout Europe. The Directive will limit the rights of copying works for personal use, through limiting the scope of fair use. Further, the Directive introduces the concept of protection of technical measures for anti-copying. Such anti-circumvention provisions were debated in the U.S. during the enactment of the federal

---

11   See http://www.creativecommons.org/.

law Digital Millennium Copyright Act. The anti-circumvention provisions are said to limit the possibilities of research and also to limit otherwise legal fair-use. The debate is further spurred by confusion as to whether the acquisition of a copy of a copyrighted work is a right to access the work in a certain way designated by the copyright proprietor or a right to the copy as such with free access rights – in any way the holder of the copy may choose. Meanwhile, the patents are expanding into copyright, in particular when it comes to computer programs. This provides problems for developers who may no longer develop any technical solution to a certain problem without being subjected to possible patent infringement.

Historically, legislators has been wary of regulating the private sphere and did not recognise a need for doing so. For example, some ten years ago, when the Swedish Copyright Act was revised, this was still the position held by the legislators. They were aware of the common practice among friends of copying and distributing mix tapes of favourite songs. Swedish legislators reasoned that it was not a good thing to try to regulate the private sphere, since the legislation would be very hard to enforce. In regulation, one should try to refrain from creating rules that cannot be enforced, since they erode the populace's confidence and trust in the law as something logical and beneficial to society. But the digitalisation of copyright and the Internet have made it much easier to obtain control over and monitor copyright violation, even if such activities are conducted in the private sphere.

The only thing that is certain in this hard-to-navigate landscape is that the protection of ideas and expressions is being expanded. Depending on your current position, you may like or dislike it, but the last word concerning intellectual property rights on the Internet has yet to be uttered.

5 Intellectual property law and ownership in employment relationships

Sanna Wolk

5.1 Introduction

There are different types of intellectual property, such as trademarks, patents for inventions, design of industrial products, copyright and neighbouring rights. Nowadays many companies are well aware of the value of intellectual property. The ownership and control of intellectual property rights is crucial to the success of any business and in order to maximise the value of intellectual property assets it is necessary to maintain and effectively manage all of their associated ownership rights.

Intellectual property is created by various groups of persons, which can include contractors, employees or sub-contracted manpower. Most frequently, however, development, research and creative activities are still performed by employees.

> Traditionally, companies' most important assets were limited to fixed assets, such as land, real property, machines and equipment, and similar. Even though manpower has always been regarded as essential for a business, it has also been considered replaceable. Employees could be replaced without jeopardising the company and its future. However, in our service-oriented, technologically innovative economy, human capital, such as key persons with know-how and creative ideas regarding a company's products and services, is a valued asset.

Recent decades have brought an upsurge of interest in the legal ownership of intellectual property rights created by employees. This interest is reflected in international discussions from the beginning of the 1900s onwards. However, there are no international solutions regarding employees' intellectual property rights. At present the nature of both employees' and employers' rights is defined by national legislation. Furthermore, there is no standard formula for the employers' right at national level.[1] In some countries the relevant rules on the employer's right to employees' intellectual assets are to be found in the national intellectual property acts. In other countries and for certain intellectual property rights, a transfer from the employee to the employer follows from general principles of law. Consequently, the methods of identifying the owner of, and establishing rights over an employee's intellectual property assets, are relatively uncertain. Therefore, in our global economy with cross border research and development, clarification of these questions in the employment contract or within a specific contract could be useful to both parties.

5.2   Different approaches in different law systems

From a legal perspective, the view on the right of employers to employees' intellectual rights differs substantially between the two main legal systems in the world today, the common law system and the civil law system. This apart from those legal systems based on Asian and Arab-Islamic cultures.

In the *common law system*,[2] e.g. in the United States and in the United Kingdom, the investor (employer) benefits from its employees' intellectual creations. The situation is similar in the Netherlands. In those countries the employer is the initial owner of the employees' intellectual property rights produced in the course of the employment. The employer is treated as the first owner, but not deemed to be the author. Therefore the duration of copyright, for example, is measured with reference to the life of the employed cre-

---

1   *See further* the AIPPI Committee Report No, Q183 on Employers' Rights to Intellectual Property at http://www.aippi.org/.
2   Otherwise called the Anglo-Saxon system.

ator. Further on, the national laws in these countries make it clear that contractual provisions, whether expressed or implied, can affect the employer's initial ownership.

In the *civil law system*,[3] to which most of the countries of Continental Europe – Germany, France and the Nordic countries, for example – belong, a legal person such as an employer, may not generally be deemed the first holder of an intellectual property right. Those rights are normally linked to individual persons. Therefore, an employer may normally only obtain intellectual property rights by assignment by law or in contract.

5.3 Ownership and harmonisations efforts at a European level

At present no major international harmonisation efforts are in progress regarding employees' intellectual property rights. The ownership and control of intellectual property rights are mainly managed in national legislation. However, within the European Union, the Commission has, from the 1970s onwards, adopted and is continuing to introduce a number of measures which seek to harmonise ownership aspects of employee's intellectual property rights throughout the Union.

5.3.1 Employees' inventions

During the 1970s an effort was made in the patent field to adopt a Community Patent Convention, a convention that has not yet come into operation. Patent protects new inventions, involving an inventive step, insofar they are capable of industrial application, as for example software inventions.

At that time, in the 1970s, the opinion within the European Community was that matters regarding employees' inventions should be dealt with under the Member States' national laws and not harmo-

3   Otherwise called the Roman-Germanic or written law system.

nised at a European level.[4] The need for harmonisation in the field of employees' inventions was not considered an urgent matter, hence the differences in the laws of the Member States. Since then, during the 1990s and 2000s, the European Commission has announced that possible harmonisation as regards inventions by employees is not necessary and that the matter should continue to be regulated by the various national laws.[5]

Today, at a national level, the rights to employees' inventions are regulated to a greater extent than the rights to other intellectual property assets created by employees. For instance, Austria, Belgium, Cyprus, the Czech Republic, Denmark, Estonia, Finland, France, Germany, Greece, Hungary, Italy, Latvia, Lithuania, Malta, the Netherlands, Poland, Portugal, Slovenia, Spain, Sweden and the United Kingdom all have national provisions on the ownership of employee's inventions.

5.3.2 Employees' copyright

In the late 1980s and in the early 1990s, copyright was at the centre of attention within the European Union. Copyright protects creations of the mind insofar they are original and expressed in a particular form. Copyright protection covers a very broad range of creations, such as software, databases, web pages and multimedia works.

---

4   *Compare* Article 60(1) of the European Patent Convention (EPC). EPC has left patent ownership to the discretion of the states signatory to it and the right to a European patent is determined in accordance with the law of the State in which the employee is mainly employed. If the State in which the employee is mainly employed cannot be determined, the law to be applied will be that of the State in which the employee's employer has his place of business. *See also* Article 11(4) of the Regulation (EC) No 2100/94 on Community Plant Variety Rights. From the provision it follows that if the breeder is an employee, the entitlement to the Community plant variety right shall be determined in accordance with the national law applicable to the employment relationship in the context of which the variety was bred, or discovered and developed.

5   *See further* the Green Paper on the Community Patent and the Patent System in Europe, COM(97) 314 final and the Proposal for a Council Regulation on the Community Patent COM(2000) 412 final.

In the late 1980s the European Commission published its proposals for copyright within the Community.[6] The Commission's efforts led among other to the adoption of Directive 91/250/EEC on the Legal Protection of Computer Programs. Article 2(3) of the Directive contains a mandatory requirement on employees' programs.[7] The employer shall exclusively be entitled to exercise all *economic rights* in an employee's computer program, where a program is created in the execution of the employee's duties or where the employee is following instructions given by the employer.[8] It is an automatic legal transfer of the copyright in computer programs. However, if the parties agree, the employed author of the computer program can recover the rights through a specific clause in the employment contract or a separate agreement on the exploitation of the computer program made by the employee (waiving the legal automatic transfer of rights).

A similar provision to Article 2(3) of the Directive on Computer Programs was included in the first draft of the Directive 96/9/EC on the Legal Protection of Databases. However, it was deleted from the final version of the Directive and recital 29 only states that nothing prevents Member States from stipulating in national laws that where a database is created by an employee in the execution of the duties or following the instructions given by the employer, the employer exclusively shall be entitled to exercise the rights in the database so created. Yet, during early 2000s the European Commission

---

6   *See* the Green Paper on Copyright and the Challenge of Technology – Copyright Issues Requiring Immediate Action, COM(88) 172 final and the Follow-up to the Green Paper – Working Programme of the Commission in the field of Copyright and Neighbouring Rights, COM(90) 584 final.

7   Article 2 of the Directive on Computer Programs deals with authorship of programs, collective works and employees' works. Article 2(1) sets out that the author of a computer program is the natural person or group of natural persons who have created the program or, where the legislation of the Member States permits, the legal person designated as the rightholder. Where collective works are recognised by national legislation the person considered by the laws of the Member State to have created the work will be deemed its author. From article 2(2) it follows that where a computer program is created by a group of natural persons co-operating together, the exclusive rights will be owned jointly. However, this means that Member States having jurisdiction and neither recognising that corporations can be authors, nor recognising the concept of collective works, do not have to change their laws.

8   *Compare* Article 3(2)a Directive 87/54/EEC on the Legal Protection of Topographies of Semiconductor Products (a non-mandatory provision regarding employees' chips).

---

has announced as regards ownership of employees copyright that: "At this point, it would seem advisable to analyse the issue further and, in particular, identify specific situations where harmonisation would yield added value and address Internal Market needs."[9]

Summing up, today only employee's computer programs are regulated at European level and the question of employees' copyrighted works in general is left to national legislation. In some countries, such as in the Netherlands and the United Kingdom, national copyright acts regulated employees' copyright. In other countries, such as Germany, France and the Nordic countries, a transfer from the employee to the employer follows from general principles of law. Nevertheless, all Member States have included in their national copyright laws provisions implementing the mandatory requirement on employees' computer programs in Article 2(3) of the Directive on Computer Programs.[10] *Moral rights*, however, such as right of paternity and right of integrity, are left outside the scope of the Computer Program Directive and are therefore currently regulated by national provisions.[11] In the Member States belonging to the civil law system, moral rights are considered to arise directly in the author and to be inalienable even by voluntary transfer (cession) to an employer. On the other hand, in the Member States belonging to the common law system, employees have no moral rights as the copyright is vested in the employer.[12] Yet, the employer normally does not have a right to the moral rights.

---

9   Commission Staff Working Paper on the Review of the EC Legal Framework in the Field of Copyright and Related Rights, SEC(2004) 995, Brussels, 19.7.2004 p. 14.

10 *See further* the Report from the Commission to the Council, the European Parliament and the Economic and Social Committee on the implementation and effects of Directive 91/250/EEC on the Legal Protection of Computer Programs, COM(2000) 199 final.

11 *See also* Article 6*bis* of the Berne Convention for the Protection of Literary and Artistic Works of 1886.

12 *See e.g.* Sections 79(3) and 82(1) the United Kingdom Copyright, Designs and Patents Act of 1988 on employee's copyright, Section 40(a) of the Swedish Copyright Act of 1960 and Section 59 of the Danish Copyright Act of 1993 on employees' computer programs. Nevertheless, it is questionable if these provisions are in line with Article 6*bis* of the Berne Convention.

5.3.3   Employees' designs

The protection of industrial designs is growing in importance. A design is the ornamental or aesthetic aspect of an article. Designs are applied to a great variety of products from different industry and trade sectors, from complex instruments with a special or exclusive use, such as machines, vehicles, tools, computers, to simple or everyday articles, such as clothes, electrical appliances, toys and furniture.

In the 1990s, after having dealt with patents and with selected areas of copyright, the European Commission turned its attention to the harmonisation of industrial designs within the Community.[13] The first effort was the adoption of Directive 98/71/EC on the Legal Protection of Designs. However, since ownership of rights in design is an area where the laws of Member States differ, there is no provision in the Directive dealing with employees' designs.[14] Nevertheless, since 2002 there is a Community-wide right of design protection. This was established through Regulation 6/2002/EC on Community Designs. The Regulation is binding in its entirety and directly applicable in all Member States since 6th March 2002. As to Community design, all design rights are automatically vested in the employer, where the design is developed in the execution of the employee's duties or when the employee is following instructions given by the employer. This follows from Article 14(3) of the Regulation.[15] However, this unless otherwise agreed or specified under national law. As a design right is intended to be an economic right, rather than a moral one, a transfer of a design can therefore be total (compare with copyright).

---

13   *See* the Green Paper on the Legal Protection of Industrial Design (III/F/5131/91).
14   The Green Paper on the Legal Protection of Industrial Design made elaborate provision for employee designs a provision that was based on Article 60(1) of the EPC. Yet, the provision was abandoned in the initial 1993 Draft Proposal.
15   Article 14 of the Design Regulation sets out who will be the first owner of a design, of a jointly made design and an employee's design. From Article 14(1) it follows that the right to the Community design shall be vested in the designer or the designer's successor in title. If two or more persons have jointly developed a design, the right to the Community design shall be vested in them jointly, Article 14(2).

In terms of ownership of employee's designs, then, we have to distinguish between national design protection, valid only within the Member State's territory, and Community design protection, that provides right holders with a right which is valid throughout the European Union. However, Community design can be available next to a Member State's national design, especially during the short period of unregistered design and national registered design. In practice it can happen that there is a clear provision on employees' Community design, but no national provision, or a conflicting one, regarding the transfer of national design rights from the employee to the employer. The Design Regulation does not declare whether the Community provisions on employees' design or national law should prevail in those situations.

One more cautionary note is in order. Since a design can also be protected by copyright, in those situations national provisions on copyright may be applicable at the same time as the provisions in the Design Regulation. National provisions that do not always stipulate the same as in Article 14(3) of the Design Regulation.

5.4 Conclusion

Summing up, there is no international harmonisation in the matter of ownership of intellectual property rights. National laws still vary to a great extent from country to county, and each intellectual property right is based on whether or not the applicable legislation provides guidance. Nevertheless, similarities also exist between the national legislations concerning ownership of employees' intellectual property rights created during the course of employment. Furthermore, one common thread for all intellectual property areas is that a properly drafted agreement can help ensure that the party seeking ownership of the relevant intellectual property rights will get what it bargained for and secure the value of its intellectual property assets.

I have now briefly described the legal situation concerning employees' intellectual assets. The last issue I would like to address is whether uniform rules in this field are desirable at an international, or at least at a European, level. It is a challenging question, today at the beginning of the twenty-first century. My opinion is that it would be desirable. Particularly as the existence of differences between national laws concerning employers' and employees' rights to intellectual property causes complications and problems for cross-border research and development, both within multinational enterprises and for co-operation between companies. Divergent rules concerning employees and employers' rights create uncertainty. Furthermore, intellectual property rights have shown an increasing tendency to overlap, and a given object of intellectual creativity may be covered by several and perhaps as regads ownership, conflicting rights.

However, there are a number of questions that have to be considered before it is possible to create uniform international, or European, rules regarding employers' rights to employees' intellectual creations.[16] Nevertheless, in the work with uniform rules, it is important to find a proper balance between the interests of the employee and the employer and a reward to employees may be fair. Especially when some employed creators, depending on what intellectual property rights are created, are economically compensated through mandatory national provisions for the rights that are transferred to the employer. For instance several European Member States have mandatory provisions regarding employed inventors' right to reasonable remuneration for the rights in inventions transferred to the employer. This applies for instance in the Czech Republic, Denmark, France, Finland, Germany, Greece, Hungary, Italy, the Netherlands, Portugal, Spain, Sweden and the United Kingdom. For other intellectual creations, national solutions vary as regards the employed creator's right to economic compensation and there is no European homogeneity. Nevertheless, it is important to have fair and coherent principles applicable to all intellectual property rights.

---

16 *See also* the AIPPI Resolution of the Q183 on Employers' Rights to Intellectual Property at http://www.aippi.org/.

- The ownership of employee's intellectual assets can be laid down in a contract, e.g. in the employment contract or in a separate contract.
- In the absence of any particular contractual clause, there is no international guidance that provides for specific solutions regarding employee's intellectual property rights.
- The ownership and control of intellectual property rights are mainly managed in national legislation. However, at a national level there is no standard formula for the employers' right.
- Within the European Union, the Commission has adopted and is continuing to introduce a number of measures which seek to harmonise ownership aspects of employee's intellectual property rights throughout the Union.

6 Designing a legal interface for contracting on the Internet

Christina Ramberg

6.1 Introduction

Law is about the rules of the game. The rules decide how we are supposed to act and the consequences if we do not act in accordance with the rules. The rules in society are to a large extent decided by national parliaments in legislation. In commerce, however, the parties themselves can decide the rules of the game by agreeing on contractual terms. When the parties have decided the rules of the game for themselves there is less need to resort to national law. This chapter mainly deals with how such agreements can be made in an Internet setting.

It should be clarified already at the outset that there is a great difference between Business-to-Business (B2B) transactions and Business-to-Consumer (B2C) transactions. For B2C transactions the national legislators have generally enacted protective legislations limiting the possibilities for the parties to agree on terms and conditions to the consumers' detriment. Legislation that limits the freedom of contract is called mandatory legislation.

Although B2B transactions are rather free in the sense that the parties can decide the rules of the game for themselves, there are limitations in national law. The limitations vary from one jurisdiction to another, and thus it sometimes becomes important to connect a transaction to a certain jurisdiction. National law also becomes relevant in situations where the parties have not totally regulated their rules of the game, since it supplements the contractual relationship with "default rules", i.e. law that provides solutions to problems unless the parties themselves have agreed on other rules.

Initially the Internet was perceived as a lawless paradise where no national law applied. However, it has turned out to be the exact opposite, with many jurisdictions applying simultaneously to one and the same transaction. Several states may claim that their legal rules should govern a transaction and when the law differs in different states, the parties may face enormous problems in adhering to many conflicting rules. In B2B transactions the parties may decide which jurisdiction that is applicable but in B2C transactions this possibility is largely limited. Furthermore it should be noted that not even the parties in a B2B transaction are free to agree upon the applicable law in relation to marketing, taxes and insolvency.

Law is about the interface. If parties want to set the rules of the game for themselves it is important that the rules are made known to them. If a process is automated and things occur automatically "behind the screens", it has no legal relevance. The important matter is how the transactions and the effects *appear* for the *users*. This chapter seeks to show how an Internet website should be designed in order to establish the wanted legal effects. This includes not only the actual design of web pages but also the content of membership terms and other sources of information to the users.

6.2 The contractual parties

Many parties may be involved in an e-commerce transaction. We have the "constructors" of the website (experts in logistics, programming, design and marketing) who may contract with a website holder (the seller or the marketplace operator), who in turn may have contractual arrangements with an Internet operator (ISP) and a server host. The user (the person interacting with the website, for example a buyer) may establish a contractual relationship with the website holder, but before doing so he or she already must have a contractual relationship with an Internet operator (ISP) and before that a contract with someone selling him or her the computer and/ or mobile phone. In order to ship the product sold at the website (if it is a physical product) there must be companies involved to transport the goods. And in order to make the payment credit card companies, banks and escrow agents may have contracts with both the webpage holder and the user.

This was only a short example of the many parties involved in an e-commerce transaction. There can be many more. From a legal point of view it is vital to understand who has a contract with whom. Normally there are only two parties to one contract. These parties may then in turn have contracts with other parties. But each contract normally only consists of two parties. The reason why it is so important to identify the contracting parties to an individual contract is that a party may normally only direct a claim against his own contracting party. If, for example, a user of a website was induced to make a mistake due to a misleading interface produced by an independent webmaster, the user cannot direct a claim directly against the webmaster. The user should direct his claim towards the website holder, with whom the user has a contractual relationship. The website holder may then in turn direct a claim towards his contractual party, the webmaster.

In practice it is sometimes unclear who has a contract with whom. A quite common example is the consumer having a contractual agreement with a net operator (a phone company) whereby he or she undertakes to pay for all calls from his telephone number. If this phone connection is linked to a computer with Internet access, the consumer must pay for the Internet traffic to the net operator (for example per minute or as a fixed fee per month). But when the consumer gets access to the Internet he or she may make many transactions with other parties than the net operator. He or she may for example buy a book at Amazon.com. The buyer concludes a contract with Amazon.com that is wholly independent of the contract with the net operator. Amazon.com cannot refer to the contract between the consumer and the net operator when claiming payment from the consumer. Amazon.com can only rely on the contract established when the consumer visited Amazon.com's website.

6.3   Binding agreements

A contract is concluded when the parties agree to be bound and to perform their obligations. After the contract is concluded the parties are not free to change their minds, but instead are obliged to stick to the deal. Normally it is implicit that the seller undertakes to deliver and that the buyer undertakes to pay, and consequently the exact moment in time when a contract is concluded can be difficult to ascertain. In an electronic setting, however, this moment can be decided quite easily if the website has a clear point of no return. In other words, an icon stipulating that if you click here, you are bound to perform xxx and entitled to get zzz and you may not change your mind afterwards. The more clearly this is communicated to the user, the more probable it is that the law in any state considers the transaction to be a binding contract.

6.3.1 Cooling-off periods

For some transactions national law provides a mandatory cooling-off period, or a time limit within which both parties or one party may change their mind and terminate the contract. This is particularly frequent in Internet consumer sales, where the consumer is entitled to a one week or two week cooling-off period. In Europe the Distance Selling Directive 97/7/EC has forced all member states to enact such legislation. Unfortunately, the Directive is differently implemented in the different states, but by and large they all allow for a two-week cancellation period. The consumer must be informed of his right to terminate the contract and the cancellation period does not normally start to run until such information is given to the consumer. Consequently it is vital to provide such information at the website in connection with the transaction being finalised. There are a number of exceptions from the mandatory cooling-off period, for example for transactions at auctions, for travels, unsealed music and literature, concerts and sporting events. Furthermore, the cooling-off period is not applicable if the product sold is naturally evanescent, such as food. Of course the consumer cannot return products that have been used. The extent to which the consumer is obliged to pay for the costs of returning the product to the seller varies.

For a business setting up Internet sales to consumer on a worldwide basis, it is important to check to what extent there are mandatory cooling-off provisions and to either obey by the law that is most favourable to the consumer or to tailor a specific interface for each jurisdiction adapted to the consumer protection laws of each jurisdiction.

In B2B there is normally no mandatory law about cooling-off periods. However, it is not uncommon that the parties agree on a cooling-off period. This can be a way of enhancing trust in a seller's products. If nothing is said about cooling-off periods before the contract is concluded, none of the parties can terminate the contract without a good reason (such as the product being defective or delivered too late). If the other party accepts a termination it is of course possible to terminate.

With C2C (consumer-to-consumer) transactions too, there is generally no law that allows for mandatory cooling-off periods. If one of the parties wishes to have a possibility of returning the product, he or she should make sure that the other party agrees to such a right of cancellation before the contract is concluded.

6.3.2   Form requirements

There are great differences in the world regarding the extent to which the law requires a contract to be formalised or not. Some states (US and EU) take as a point of departure that there are no formal requirements and then make exceptions for certain transactions (for example the sale of real estate, credit loans to consumers and the sale of high-value products). Other jurisdictions generally require contracts to be in writing (China). When setting up a webpage for e-commerce it is important to check to what extent formal requirements exist in the states that the webpage is meant to be used in.

One problem in relation to formal requirements is whether electronic documents constitute "writing" and whether the requirement of a signature can be satisfied by an electronic signature (see more about electronic signatures in chapter 8). In many international analyses it has been established that "writing" is anything that can be saved and understood, which would normally include electronic documents. Law and judges, however, are conservative by nature and simply because something is logically true, it need not be legally relevant. In many jurisdictions it is unfortunately still highly uncertain whether an electronic document would satisfy a legal requirement of writing. In sensitive high-value transactions it is probably still best to verify the transaction by paper-and-ink technique when there is a legal requirement of writing. Some states, however, explicitly accept electronic documents as equivalent to writing (for instance Canada and the USA).

Other formal requirements may stipulate that certain information must be given before the contract is concluded. Such information – for example about VAT number, the parties' addresses and suchlike – can be provided in electronic form on the webpage. It is recommended that the user explicitly confirm, by clicking in a certain box, that he or she has had the opportunity of reading particularly important information.

6.4   Terms and conditions

The rules of the game in relation to e-commerce transactions can be divided in two major parts: (1) how a contract is concluded and (2) the terms of the concluded contract. A related issue is (3) how to incorporate the rules of the game into the contractual relationship.

6.4.1   How a contract is concluded, the simple case

In the simple case, a seller offers products at his website and the buyer accepts the offer by clicking on an icon stating that the buyer is finally bound. However, even this simple case is complicated. Is the seller bound to sell when the buyer has clicked the final icon? Or can the seller reject the sale? The answer to this question varies between different jurisdictions and should consequently be clarified at the website. The seller is sometimes anxious to retain the possibility to reject the deal and can often do so by for example stipulating that he or she shall not be bound until he or she has confirmed the deal in an e-mail.

6.4.2   How a contract is concluded, the auction

Some marketplaces use more sophisticated methods of connecting sellers and buyers. It is particularly common for procurement (either by official authorities or by companies) to be set up so that buyers provide sellers with an opportunity to communicate bids. The buyers puts up the question "who can sell me xyz cheapest ?" and the sellers respond by submitting bids. This is sometimes called a reverse auction.

Traditional English auctions whereby a seller asks for bids from buyers are also quite frequently used at Internet marketplaces. Another version is the Dutch auction, where the bidding starts at a high price and then decreases at a certain pace and the buyers are requested to announce at what level they are interested in buying. In the Japanese auction, bids are submitted simultaneously. There are many other methods of conducting auctions.[1] Whatever the method used, it is important to clarify the rules of the game in more detail. The designer of the marketplace must ask him- or herself what kind of rules he or she wants to apply and then let these rules be known to the users. Here is a list of questions that may be addressed:

1 How to provide an offer.
2 When to provide an offer.
3 How to provide a bid.
4 When to provide a bid.
5 The time the auction is held.
6 The time the auction lasts (if being a time-interval-auction).
7 The opportunity to inspect the object before the auction is held.
8 To what extent the operator has the right to offer goods owned by him or her.
9 The amount the bid covers (can a bidder choose to only buy a part of the lot?) Is a bid only for a single object even if more than one is included in the lot?
10 The right to withdraw and revoke a bid.
11 The right to cancel a completed deal.
12 The right of the invitor to state a reserve price: no such right/ a duty to disclose the reserve price/ a duty to disclose that a reserve price exists/ no duty to disclose the existence of an allowed reserve price.
13 The right to withdraw an offered lot.
14 The right for the invitor to bid anonymously or by disclosing his identity or not at all.
15 The right for the operator to advance bids at his discretion.

---

1   See for instance Ramberg, Christina, *Internet Marketplaces the Law of Auctions and Exchanges Online*, Oxford University Press, 2002.

113

16 The right for the operator to advance bids on behalf of the invitor.
17 If a bid may be rejected when the advance is too small.
18 Any stipulation of the bids being automatically increased or decreased by a certain amount.
19 How the 'winning' bidder is determined.
20 What the winning bidder should pay.
21 Who pays what fees to the operator, including responsibility for taxes related to the auction.
22 Consequences where necessary permissions are not granted.
23 The applicable law.

6.4.3   The terms of the contract

The checklist above relates to how a contract is formed. Another issue is to regulate the obligations of each party once the contract is formed. This is normally contained in national sales law and can be deviated from in B2B contracts. For B2C transactions there is often mandatory national law limiting the parties' freedom to allocate risks. The following checklist provides a number of issues that should be considered.

1 The passing of the title to the goods.
2 Payment conditions: when, how and where, deposit requirements, liability for taxes, effects of failure of compliance.
3 The quality of the goods: grading standards, goods sold 'as is', 'in perfect condition', 'with all faults and errors of description', 'as and where they lie', with express warranties.
4 The liability of the operator for defects.
5 Claims must be submitted when and where and how and what is the effect of a late or wrongful claim.
6 Delivery of the goods: transport from where and to where, at whose expense and on whose responsibility.
7 Assumption of risk: from when? The fall of the hammer, the storage of the goods, the delivery of the goods.
8 The applicable law.

6.4.4 How to incorporate the rules of the game into the contractual relationship

As we have already seen, it is important to make the rules of the game available to the users. From a strictly legal point of view the conditions of sale are readily available when placed on the website below a heading at the bottom of the homepage. The reason why it may not be enough to make the terms and conditions of sale available on the website is that it is quite easy technically to determine that the participants are notified *expressly* about the existence of the terms and conditions. It is recommended that procedures be introduced whereby each user expressly accepts the terms and conditions.

From a technical point of view there are a number of procedural options for the incorporation of standard terms:

1 The user could be required to read the text of the terms and conditions of sale and certify that he or she has read and understood them. In this alternative the text is shown on the user's screen and there is no way of concluding the deal unless the whole text has been scrolled through and actively accepted (by, for instance, clicking OK in a box stating that 'I have read the terms and conditions of sale and I accept them').
2 The user could be provided with an opportunity to read the terms and conditions of sale, but the technical design is not such that the user necessarily has to read or scroll through the texts. He or she may choose to read them by clicking on a link to the text. The user must actively accept the terms by clicking in a box on the screen.
3 The user could be given the opportunity of reading the terms and conditions of sale and the website could state that they are incorporated, but the user does not have to read them or scroll through them, nor must he or she actively accept them.

Naturally, there are many combinations available of these three main alternatives to incorporation of standard terms in the electronic setting. When the user is likely to interact repetitively with the website, it is many times efficient to make him or her become a "member" and to use the first of the above three alternatives. Since the terms are incorporated only once in connection with the membership procedure and intended to apply to all future transactions made in the marketplace, the extra time that this alternative entails is not a major obstacle. The benefit of choosing the first alternative is that in B2B transactions at least it is fairly likely that all national jurisdictions will deem the incorporation procedure sufficient. For other situations where the user is not likely to return often to the website, it is probably better to use the second alternative. It should, however, be noted that this procedure may not be accepted by all jurisdictions as a sufficient means of incorporation.

The problem of incorporation of terms is closely connected with interpretation of the terms. Even when the terms and conditions of sale taken as a whole are deemed incorporated, there is a risk of certain clauses not being properly incorporated. Surprisingly burdensome or unusual terms may need special attention in order to be incorporated. In the traditional paper transaction, case law in different jurisdictions shows that courts are sometimes reluctant to enforce surprisingly burdensome or unusual clauses in standardised contractual texts. Also, the terms and conditions of sale for Internet transactions are standardised and may thus require special attention to be paid to unusual or burdensome clauses. This is particularly so when all or some of the users are consumers. Particular attention could be drawn to surprising or burdensome terms, for instance by repeating such clauses and having the user specifically accept these terms by individually clicking an acceptance box in relation to every such burdensome or surprising term.

6.5   Mistakes and input errors

Many users of electronic means of communication have experienced the speed at which Internet transactions are made. Maybe many have also experienced how easily it happens that something can go wrong. The "send-button" is clicked on too early, the "Yes, I accept-box" is clicked on by mistake and a kilogram of peppers is ordered instead of one piece of pepper. Worse things may also happen: One of my students working in a bank office once ordered 10,000 Ericsson shares at the Stock Exchange instead of ordering Ericsson shares to the value of 10,000 Swedish Crowns (approximately 1,000 Euros). The problem with mistakes of expression is closely related to the situation when a party becomes bound by a contract without having the intention to be bound. It is crucial that the intention to be bound in electronic transactions is properly secured. It is likewise important to prevent mistakes in expressions.

The problem of mistake has a long legal history. It has proved difficult to strike the balance between, on the one hand, the interest of a mistaken party in not being bound by unintended expressions of promises and, on the other hand, the interest of a party relying on a promise in being able to act on it. Traditionally, the risk of mistake has been placed upon the party making a mistake, the rationale being that such a rule creates an incentive to act carefully and prevent mistakes from being communicated. Another explanation for the rule is that the party to whom the mistake is communicated should be protected since it has no means of discovering the mistake. At the outset it may seem unfair to hold someone to a mistake. However, a party relying on the mistake incurs a loss and should be entitled to compensation. This is particularly the case when there was no mistake, but merely a change of mind. In practice, it is often hard to know whether a party who claims that it has made a mistake really did so or only changed its mind. In this regard, there are two major problems: First, how can it be established that it was a mistake and not merely a change of mind? Second, the suitability of allocating the risk of mistake to the relying party depends on the type of contract and on how soon the mistake is discovered and brought to the other party's attention.

For some types of contracts, it is in practice not critical if a party changes his mind and wishes to cancel a contract or withdraw an offer or bid, particularly not when notice of the mistake is provided at an early stage. In other words, when a party makes a mistake and soon after informs the other party about it, the other party does not necessarily incur any losses; this is for example the case with the sale of consumer products such as cars, bikes, kitchen appliances and the like. For such situations, it may seem unreasonably harsh to hold the promisor to his mistaken expression.

For other types of contracts it is absolutely vital that the parties be able to trust expressions of promises. This is the case, for example, at auctions and exchanges and with the sale of products exposed to rapid price variations, such as stocks, securities and commodities. If there were an opportunity to escape such contracts by referring to a mistake, parties would be tempted to refer to a mistake when they had simply made a bad bargain (the buyer could claim to have made a mistake when prices fall after the purchase). If such contracts were not upheld due to mistake, the party relying on the promise would make losses, which is not a proper risk allocation since he or she was not at fault and had no means of protecting him- or herself from the mistake made by the other party.

A third type of contract is for example those where an object that is not exposed to rapid price variations causes a party to bind him- or herself to other contracts (with sub-contractors, or suppliers) or in other ways to take passive action (such as not committing him- or herself to another contract due to the first contract making him or her fully booked). It is difficult to uphold a strict borderline between transactions that are sensitive to mistakes and transactions that are not.

Two of the main features of electronic communication are speed and automation. Both these features increase the risks of making mistakes that cannot be easily corrected before they reach the addressee and before the addressee takes actions in reliance of the mistake. Discussions in the legal literature and recent initiatives by legislative bodies indicate that there may be reason in the case of electronic commerce to adjust the present distribution of liability in connection with mistake and to take the mistaken party's need of protection into account. This trend of imposing less liability on a party making mistakes in expression (input errors) can be found in the European E-Commerce Directive[2] and in the US Uniform Electronic Transaction Act.

In designing a website for e-commerce it is important to use methods whereby input errors by the website holder are minimised. It is furthermore advisable to state in the terms that mistakes made by the website holder are not binding on him or her. It is also advisable to create a design whereby input errors from the users are prevented. This can be done fairly easily by repeating the terms of the transaction before the final "I-accept icon" is clicked on and by ensuring that the final icon is not misleading but clearly indicates to

---

2   Directive 2000/31/EC of the European parliament and Council of 8 June 2000 on certain legal aspects of information society services, in particular electronic commerce, in the Internal Market (Directive on electronic commerce).

the user that by clicking there he or she will be finally bound. Another efficient way of preventing mistakes is to use a system that is able to detect unusual behaviour and put "whether-this-really-is-what-you-want questions" to the users.

6.6   Concluding remark

In setting up a scheme for doing e-commerce, it is important to first identify the rules of the game. The legal work related to setting up an e-commerce website is not only a matter of adhering to mandatory legislation, it is mainly a question of seeing the legal dimension in the business model. Secondly, it is important to make the rules of the game known to the users. They must become aware of how they are supposed to act and what the consequences are of different actions. The most efficient method of making the rules known to the users is to design an instructive interface. This could be supplemented by texts explaining the rules of the game for the few users that have the time and energy to read such texts.

7 E-procurement

Nicklas Lundblad

7.1 Introduction

Public and private procurement are important elements in almost all economies today. Information and communication technologies are quickly changing the landscape for procurement, and new platforms, technologies, contractual structures and trading patterns force companies to reconsider their traditional ways of doing business.[1]

A major part of this reconsideration should be focussed on legal issues. The law surrounding procurement solutions is not a single unified legal topic, but rather a patchwork of diverse laws, regulations and contracts. In addition to this there are strict laws concerning one of the most important forms of procurement – public procurement – that have to be both well understood and applied to ensure that solutions are in accordance with what the law requires.

This chapter raises some of the issues that may be met with in projects concerning electronic procurement, and does so from an all-inclusive perspective – that is, with an enumeration of relevant legal areas as well as some specific problems, in order to sketch the complexity of this set of problems. So this chapter is not chiefly a theoretical analysis of procurement law, but rather an exploration of the different issues that can face the IT professional in designing e-procurement systems and as such the aim is to show the reader that the project of designing e-procurement platforms is a techno-legal task of some complexity. However, at the end we mention some of the changes in European procurement law.

---

1   *See* for an introduction e.g. Thompson, M., A. Lawson, et al., *E-procurement: purchasing for the Internet-based economy*, Butler Group, Hull, 2000; Neef, D., *E-procurement: from strategy to implementation*, Financial Times/Prentice Hall, Upper Saddle River, NJ, 2001; Nekolar, A.-P., *E-Procurement: Euphorie und Realität*, Springer, Berlin; Heidelberg; New York; Hongkong; London; Mailand; Paris; Tokio, 2003.

7.2   Defining e-procurement

E-procurement is not easily definable. Here we will speak of it as a *multilayered, technology-supported business solution for buying goods and services*. It should be noted that we do not define e-procurement as "buying on the Internet", even if this is often the form that e-procurement does take. The reason for this is that we see more or less closed e-procurement solutions as possible, in line with what we have already seen in the electronic data interchange solutions that are still working perfectly in many cases.

Other possible definitions are:[2]

> A corporate application used by large companies to provide a single corporate portal to connect internal buyers to suppliers of indirect materials.

The limitation to large companies is questionable. One might also use a shorter and more general definition:[3]

> The acquisition of products or services through the Internet or other online channels.

The advantage of such a definition is that very few things are excluded, and a broad study of relevant phenomena can be conducted. It still seems preferable to delimit the definition to businesses, in order to discern between business-to-consumer e-commerce and e-procurement. Consumers rarely engage in procurement, and thus e-procurement is chiefly something that occurs between businesses, public agencies and other similar actors.

7.3   Factors driving e-procurement

Electronic procurement is being developed because it is perceived as a useful change in the way that companies and public entities do business today. But what, more exactly, are the big differences between electronic procurement and other forms of procurement? There are, of course, a great number of different answers to this question. Some of the important answers are:

2   http://www.verticalnet.com/technology/glossary.html.
3   http://www.unisys.com/annual/annual2000/glossary/.

- *Transparency.*[4] E-procurement creates two different types of transparency – **transactional transparency** as well as **archival transparency**. The first kind of transparency ensures that we can follow and verify all the transactions in the process of procuring. The transactions are verified, recorded and completed over a network that is accessible to the buyer and the seller, and both parties can verify what has taken place. The second kind of transparency is perhaps the more important. The possibility of returning to old procurement processes and evaluating them is important in order to evaluate the efficiency and potential corruption of the procurement function in both a company and the public sector. How is this? If we can record all procurement bids, choices and evaluations – and e-procurement makes this possible – the procurement process can be independently verified and reviewed by other parties – both public and private – to ensure that favourised buying, bribery and other factors have not affected what should be a rational, economic decision.[5]

- *Elimination of mistakes.* A qualified conjecture is that many factors that eliminate companies from the bidding process on at least public contracts today are due to trivial mistakes made by inexperienced bidders. This goes especially for small and medium-sized companies that have great difficulty in understanding and applying the often-Byzantine rules of public procurement. E-procurement promises to give at least a possible solution to this problem by eliminating these mistakes before bids are submitted. This can be done by designing in simple safeguards in the interface and bidding system used.

- *Expansion of the market.* The cross-border qualities of e-commerce or e-business[6] also apply to electronic procurement. One promise which it is hoped that the new technology will fulfil is that of cre-

---

4 One country openly stating that this is an advantage is the Philippines. *See* http://www1.worldbank.org/publicsector/egov/philippines_eproc.htm. *See,* for more on Transparency, the Centre for Democracy and Technology's transparency guide: http://www.cdt.org/egov/handbook/transparency.shtml.

5 That this is not a necessary, but only a possible solution is conceded. But the possibility of such archival transparency is an important factor in developing e-procurement solutions, and this should be recognised.

6 Sometimes we see a distinction between these terms, but here they are taken to be synonymous.

ating a single European electronic market for procurement contracts. If this is indeed realized it would significantly increase the value of cross-border public procurement; the value of which today is quite low.

- *New forms of procurement.* When we apply ICT-related business development to procurement processes we also hope to create new modes and methods of procurement. One example is the move from simple fixed price bids to auctions of different kinds. This change in the price mechanism is one simple change that is made possible by the real-time updating the web offers. Another intriguing possibility is that of combinatorial bids, where complex bids can be made for different procurement processes and shared between impromptu consortiums of small or medium sized companies.[7]

- *Efficiency.* Naturally, companies or public authorities that implement e-procurement also hope to achieve gains in terms of efficiency. These gains come from many different sources. Firstly, so-called maverick buying can be reduced by using e-procurement. Instead of ad-hoc or old-friend procurement, volume discounts can be achieved by concentrating procurement to a few sellers. Secondly, the process of procurement can be streamlined significantly. Instead of dealing with masses of paper both buyers and sellers can use the new possibilities of interface design and usability features to improve the procurement experience. Thirdly, once procurement patterns become well-known companies can produce on-demand, rather than haphazardly. This will also increase efficiency by reducing inventory costs and related inefficiencies.

- *Price competition.* It should also be noted that many buyers – public or private – hope that e-procurement will lead to a higher price pressure on sellers. This is partly a result of the factors mentioned above, but not necessarily the result of using e-procurement. It has also been shown that price pressure may well be a path that

---

7   *Trade Extensions*, a company offering technology to support combinatorial bids, present a number of case studies on its web page. See for example: http://www.tradeextensions.se/press/volvoPackCase.html.

leads to deteriorating relationships with sellers, something that in the long term may harm buyers and reduce their competitive strength.[8]

- *Relationship building.* E-procurement can also be used to integrate sellers and buyers more into each other's processes, effectively creating a stronger bond between the two – ultimately to the benefit of both parties.

These are but some of the reasons for exploring e-procurement, and it seems evident that there are other reasons that go more to the nature of goods and services in particular sectors of the economy, but this will not be explored further here. Suffice it to say that e-procurement is motivated by a number of good reasons, and thus can be expected to become more and more important as a facet of both the public and private economies.

7.3.1   A note on public and private e-procurement

From a legal standpoint it is important to differentiate between public and private e-procurement. **Private e-procurement** is mostly governed by private contracts and the rules set out in these contracts.[9] **Public e-procurement** on the other hand is governed by strict laws that have been implemented to reduce the risk of corruption and other competitive hurdles when opening the public sector to market solutions.

Looking at the statistics, we soon find that private e-procurement is growing much more quickly than public e-procurement. This is certainly due to the less cumbersome rules that apply to private e-procurement, but also to the fact that private sector companies are under heavier economic pressure to adapt to new technologies so as to remain competitive in an economy where productivity growth is becoming a major factor in deciding competitive advantage.

---

8   *See* for more on this topic Platforms, E. G. o. B. B. I. T. (2003). Final Report by The Expert Group on B2B Internet Trading Platforms.

9   And by private procurement in general I refer to transactions between buying and selling companies. Consumer aspects are left out of the following discussion.

7.4 Legal issues

7.4.1 Introduction

E-procurement is many different things to many different actors. Thus it is hard to list exhaustively all the legal issues that need to be addressed (indeed it is rarely, if ever, possible to present an exhaustive legal analysis of anything in the real world). This is partly due to the fact that e-procurement solutions can look very different in both different sectors and different countries, but it is also due to the fact that e-procurement exists in between a great number of different relevant pieces of law.

E-procurement is business. Business is complex and open to interpretations. Expect no simple answers.

In the following text the aim is to highlight and examine some questions that are not specific to, but still relevant for, e-procurement. What will soon become evident is that these questions are in many cases general and can be applied to e-commerce at large. This in no way reduces the value of our examination, and it is hoped that this general applicability will not preclude the reader from engaging with the issues as they are sketched below.

7.4.2 Privacy

Privacy issues figure largely in both legal debate and scholarship on e-commerce in particular and the information society in general. E-procurement solutions often deal with what is termed "personal data" – that is, data that can be connected to a living individual in different ways. The trivial examples are the identities of sellers and buyers, but in considering privacy issues let us examine a more complicated case.

We noted above that one of the possible advantages of e-procurement is voidance of both what is termed maverick buying and corruption. Let us examine how this translates into a legal problem. To be able to eliminate maverick buying[10] it would be necessary to examine in some detail what buyers in a company are actually doing,

---

10 A term used to refer to buying patters where an organisation or a company buys from many different sources, thus squandering any possible advantage that could be gained from bulk purchasing.

and how they are procuring (from whom). Let us take a specific example: imagine that you are asked to examine whether a certain buyer at a large company has been systematically favouring one company in procuring office supplies – regardless of the fact that this selling company is not always the one with the lowest price. You suspect that this might be the case, since the owner of the company that seems to win most procurement bids is also the brother-in-law of the buyer.

One possibility open to you is to map all the procurement deals that the suspected individual has been in charge of and to simple search the database of bids to see in how many case the winning bid has not been the bid with the lowest price. What you then find will enable you to collect evidence and support the hypothesis that the individual in question is indeed systematically favouring a company that he or she has vested interests in. Is such monitoring legal?

When formulated in this general way the question is very hard to answer. The answer will depend on a large number of different issues that have to be examined closely before a tentative answer can be given. Let us assume first that the buyer is an employee – and that there exists some sort of employment agreement between the company and the buyer. Then we face a staggering number and variety of questions.

Firstly, has the monitoring of the employees been openly admitted and advertised? If the monitoring is being conducted covertly the situation may be easier to criticise than if the fact that reviews like the one mentioned above can and will be performed is openly admitted. This goes to ensure that everyone knows what kinds of personal data about them are actually collected, and why.

Secondly, has the collection of personal data relevant to the companies' security been included in the terms of employment? If the employment contract clearly states the categories of data and forms of collection that the company uses, this may well strengthen the case that the company is openly acting only to reduce risks and costs.

Thirdly, and more difficult, are the systems designed to ensure that data collected can be connected to a certain individual or only to a certain function? In order to make sense, a review like the one above can only be performed in a system where the user is consistently forced to log in with a personal identifier and a password that is unique to that individual. Imagine instead that the identifier was the computer used – to infer that the buyer had used the computer may seem natural, but what do you present as evidence for making the link between computer and buyer? You might otherwise be collecting data on somebody else, or on several different individuals using the same computer, indiscriminately.

Many legal issues can be addressed early on, in system design, and risks reduced by designing systems to enable traceability and review! Lawrence Lessig has examined the new possibilities of building architectures with regulative effects, and shown that in many cases system architecture can be likened to law.[11]

These are some of the considerations that would have to be made in examining the case given above. As is quickly realised, cases such as these are difficult and all that can be done to proactively reduce the risks (such as admitting and advertising monitoring practices, including them in the terms of employment et cetera) is to be recommended.

There are also other considerations that must be taken into account when working with personal data. If a system is designed to log data that can later be used as evidence of wrong-doing or corruption, the security of that system has to be on a satisfactory level. System design is influenced by the rules of the so-called Data Protection Directive (95/46/EC).[12] This is worth examining in some detail, since many of the e-procurement systems are systems that deal with personal data.

Article 17 in the directive provides:

Article 17

Security of processing

1 Member States shall provide that the controller must implement appropriate technical and organizational measures to protect personal data against accidental or unlawful destruction or accidental loss, alteration, unauthorized disclosure or access, in particular where the processing involves the transmission of data over a network, and against all other unlawful forms of processing.

---

11 Lessig, L., *Code and other laws of cyberspace*, Basic Books, New York, 1999.
12 Directive 95/46/EC of the European Parliament and of the Council of 24 October 1995 on the protection of individuals with regard to the processing of personal data and on the free movement of such data.

Having regard to the state of the art and the cost of their implementation, such measures shall ensure a level of security appropriate to the risks represented by the processing and the nature of the data to be protected.

This Article has direct consequences for a company wanting to implement an e-procurement solution where personal data will be stored and processed, and there are of course few such systems completely void of personal data.[13]

If we read this first section of the article closely we find that it is broad in scope. Not only must the technical level of security be assured, the organisational level of security must also be considered. The trade-off that is proposed between the costs and the nature of the data, also considering the state of the art, does not help much, especially since the state of the art in e-procurement and information security changes quickly and unexpectedly.[14]

Companies must, however, take the section (as it is implemented in their national legal systems) into account. They should thus be ready to answer the question of how they weighed the different interests in the article and arrived at the system design they now have.

This is not a problem peculiar to e-procurement, but it is an example of a legal provision that becomes applicable to e-procurement platforms and complicates the design and operation of these platforms.[15]

It should also be noted that the security requirements still apply if the e-procurement solution is out-sourced. The rest of the article makes this obvious:

---

13 It is of course possible to build a procurement system that is completely anonymous. But then such a system may come into conflict with other laws requiring that economic data can be traced. One example would be the Sarbanmes-Oxley Act in the US, see especially sec. 404.

14 Consider the following case: your system is designed with triple-DES encryption, say, and a fundamental flaw in that form of encryption is discovered. The state of the art then changes from regarding triple-DES as secure to fundamentally insecure as a solution for encryption.

15 Why the operation? Because the security level cannot be decided once and for all. It has to be reviewed regularly.

2 The Member States shall provide that the controller must, where processing is carried out on his behalf, choose a processor providing sufficient guarantees in respect of the technical security measures and organizational measures governing the processing to be carried out, and must ensure compliance with those measures.

3 The carrying out of processing by way of a processor must be governed by a contract or legal act binding the processor to the controller and stipulating in particular that:
   – the processor shall act only on instructions from the controller,
   – the obligations set out in paragraph 1, as defined by the law of the Member State in which the processor is established, shall also be incumbent on the processor.

4 For the purposes of keeping proof, the parts of the contract or the legal act relating to data protection and the requirements relating to the measures referred to in paragraph 1 shall be in writing or in another equivalent form.

This is also important to consider in cases where a third party e-procurement service is used. The security levels and requirements cannot just be ignored in such cases, but must be explicitly referenced in the hosting contract or some other such equivalent form.[16]

These are two important aspects of privacy that apply to e-procurement platforms. The entire legal framework embodied in the Data Protection Directive is relevant to the design and use of e-procurement solutions. The point of these two examples is simply to alert the reader to the fact that privacy issues will play a part in the design of e-procurement platforms. Deeper and more detailed information on privacy law is to be found elsewhere in this book.

7.4.3 Intellectual property rights

Another important area of law often actualised by systems design is intellectual property rights of different kinds.[17] In designing e-procurement systems we face at least two kinds of different IPR-related questions.

16 Contractual agreements can naturally specify even more strict conditions.
17 For an overview and introduction *see* Koktvedgaard, M. and M. Levin, *Lärobok i immaterialrätt: upphovsrätt, patenträtt, mönsterrätt, känneteckensrätt i Sverige, EU och internationellt*, Norstedts juridik, Stockholm, 2004.

The first question is a question about the use of content[18] in designing the system. Who owns the catalogues, databases, pictures, texts and other material used in the platform? It is essential that all content used is clearly declared in terms of what rights pertain to the content in question and what licences, if any, are applicable. This can be done by listing the content of the system and determining how rights and licences can be determined. Let us look at a simple example:

Content source/ technology	Right	Owner	To do
Database of products	Database rights – *sui generis?*[19]	The company having produced the database.	Clear acceptable use licenses with owner
Pictures of the product	Copyright	Photographer.	Find photographer, and find out if the photos have been sold, or if they are only licensed
Reviews of products	Copyright	Writer	Same as above
Search technology or other similar technology	Patent?	Patent holder	Are patented technologies being used in the design of the system? Have the appropriate licenses been acquired?
Software	Copyright? Patent?	Software company?	Is all software properly licensed?

18 This term is used broadly to refer to not only text, pictures and other such content but also to software and technologies employed in the design of the system.
19 Sui generis: literally, of its own kind, or unique. This refers to the special intellectual property right defined for databases in the so-called Database Directive (Directive 96/9/EC of the European Parliament and of the Council of 11 March 1996 on the legal protection of databases).

131

These are a few of the necessary questions to ask in the design phase, and it seems obvious that asking them will reduce exposure to legal risks.[20]

The second, and perhaps more intriguing, question is how to deal with the data that an e-procurement system actually produces, rather than uses. A well-designed e-procurement system will aggregate large amounts of data assets – trading patterns, company behaviours, price levels, resiliency to price cuts, profit margins and other similar data can be divined from the long-time interactions in an e-procurement platform. These assets may well prove very valuable to the party that controls them.[21]

If the buying party can use the e-procurement system to map price sensitivity and other essential facts about the sellers, this may well mean that the seller's position will weaken considerably. If the seller, on the other hand, is able to ascertain the production needs and time restraints the buyer works under, this may work to the seller's advantage. The data produced by the e-procurement platform thus has a significant value. But who *owns* it?

This is a complicated issue and the best thing to do is to try, proactively, to ascertain what assets can be produced by the systems in terms of data sets and make sure that these are divided in a way that makes sense. By setting out terms and conditions in a contract, prior to the design of the platform, many contentious issues may be resolved more efficiently than if they have to be resolved *post factum*.

These two questions are broad and general. Still they show with sufficient force that intellectual property rights cannot be ignored when designing e-procurement systems. For a deeper and more detailed discussion on intellectual property rights, see chapter 4.

---

20 The focus on legal risks is a growing discipline in law, *see for example* Wahlgren, Peter, *Juridisk riskanalys: mot en säkrare juridisk metod,* Jure, Stockholm, 2003.
21 It is a separate but interesting observation that the *raw* data may be less interesting and that data mining technologies may have to be applied to generate interesting results. Still, the potentially interesting nature of the data produced justifies directing legal attention at data sets produced by e-procurement systems.

7.4.4   Electronic signatures

Electronic signature law[22] is also relevant to designing e-procurement platforms. Security concerns, as well as new legal provisions on corporate governance require that decisions can be monitored, reviewed and traced in a manner that encourages personal responsibility.[23] It is thus possible, even probable, that the systems used to trade with the e-procurement platform will utilise electronic signatures in some form, shape or manner. It is then important to be aware of the law on electronic signatures and what it requires from the design of the system. The European directive on electronic signatures[24], gives specific rules on liability as well as data protection that have to be closely analysed for the e-procurement solution at hand. Security and interoperability with other systems will not be easy to achieve.[25] Even to manage electronic signatures legally is far from simple.[26]

7.4.5   E-commerce law

Another important area of law is e-commerce law in general. The so-called E-commerce directive[27] contains several important legal provisions[28] which may by relevant for designing an e-procurement

---

22   It is often assumed that there is a difference between "electronic signatures" and "digital signatures". Indeed, several different distinctions between the two concepts can be introduced. Here, however, no such finery is needed.

23   Among the developments that could be mentioned we again find the Sarbanes Oxley Act, the American legislation that followed the collapse of Enron. This legislation contains numerous requirements that economic and corporate governance can be monitored and reviewed. These requirements may well have to be translated to technological fixes.

24   *See* Directive 1999/93/EC of the European Parliament and of the Council of 13 December 1999 on a Community framework for electronic signatures.

25   *See* specifically for this issue Kirchberger, Christine &Ramon y Olano, Jon, *Issues of Security and Interoperability in Electronic Public Procurement*, in Wahlgren, Peter (ed.), *IT-law*, Scandinavian Studies of Law, vol. 47, 2004.

26   *See* Magnusson-Sjöberg, Cecilia, *Managing Electronic Signatures*, in Nielsen, R, Sandfeld Jacobsen, S & Trzaskowski, J (eds), *EU Electronic Commerce Law*, Djof, 2004; *See* in this volume: Anna Nordén, *The legal potentials and pitfalls of electronic signatures*.

27   Directive 2000/31/EC of the European Parliament and of the Council of 8 June 2000 on certain legal aspects of information society services, in particular electronic commerce, in the Internal Market ('Directive on electronic commerce').

28   Even though it may be argued that this piece of legislation primarily focuses on consumer interests, it still has a cursory interest for business interactions.

---

platform. The information duties imposed on companies in this Directive are especially important to be aware of and comply with. One simple example will suffice to show this. Since e-procurement services can be outsourced or available through different forms of electronic markets, they can in some cases be regarded as "information society service providers" and thus subject to the information requirements in the directive.[29] One example is found in article 5 of the aforementioned Directive. Note that the requirements are both extensive in scope and precise in detail:

Article 5

General information to be provided

1 In addition to other information requirements established by Community law, Member States shall ensure that the service provider shall render easily, directly and permanently accessible to the recipients of the service and competent authorities, at least the following information:
(a) the name of the service provider;
(b) the geographic address at which the service provider is established;
(c) the details of the service provider, including his electronic mail address, which allow him to be contacted rapidly and communicated with in a direct and effective manner;
(d) where the service provider is registered in a trade or similar public register, the trade register in which the service provider is entered and his registration number, or equivalent means of identification in that register;
(e) where the activity is subject to an authorisation scheme, the particulars of the relevant supervisory authority;
(f) as concerns the regulated professions:
  – any professional body or similar institution with which the service provider is registered,
  – the professional title and the Member State where it has been granted,
  – a reference to the applicable professional rules in the Member State of establishment and the means to access them;
(g) where the service provider undertakes an activity that is subject to VAT, the identification number referred to in Article 22(1) of the sixth Council Directive 77/388/EEC of 17 May 1977 on the

---

29 The definition of "information society services" is broad: "any service, normally provided for remuneration, at a distance, by electronic means and at the individual request of a recipient of services".

harmonisation of the laws of the Member States relating to turnover taxes – Common system of value added tax: uniform basis of assessment(29).

2 In addition to other information requirements established by Community law, Member States shall at least ensure that, where information society services refer to prices, these are to be indicated clearly and unambiguously and, in particular, must indicate whether they are inclusive of tax and delivery costs.

The directive also contains rules on commercial communications of different kinds, as well as rules on the freedom to establish services, that can be relevant to the design of e-procurement services.[30]

7.4.6   Competition law

E-procurement, especially when conducted by private companies, may give raise to competition concerns. If the buyers on a market pool their buying, this efficiently becomes a monopsony, a buyers' monopoly.[31] There have been cases where e-procurement solutions have been discussed and analysed from the view point of competition law. The most well-known case is the large web procurement solution created by the auto industry, Covisint.[32] The US Federal Trade Commission (FTC) examined the procurement platform to see if it violated the American Clayton Act, but decided that it did not.[33] They did, however, leave open the issue of whether buying ventures such as Covisint may in the future become a problem:[34]

In notifying the parties of its action, the Commission noted that, because Covisint is in the early stages of its development and has not yet adopted bylaws, operating rules, or terms for participant access, because it is not yet operational, and because its founders represent

---

30   It is important to observe that these information duties are not obviously only required in business-to-consumer situations. Note that relevant authorities should also be able to access the information specified in the directive, and that recipients may be companies as well as individuals. There is also the issue of how to correctly identify a user as a legal representative or a consumer in a real Internet situation.

31   If the relevant market for the companies is the target for the coordinated procurement effort, and they represent a large portion of the buyers on that market.

32   *See* Covisint web site http://www.covisint.com/.

33   *See* FTC Press Release.Re: Decision to close investigation of the Covisint B2B electronic marketplace. September 11, 2000.

34   http://www.ftc.gov/opa/2000/09/covisint.htm.

135

such a large share of the automobile market, the Commission cannot say that implementation of the Covisint venture will not cause competitive concerns. In view of this, the Commission reserved the right to take such further action as the public interest may require.

It is easy to see that collaboration around an e-procurement platform will have to be carefully tailored to avoid competition concerns from relevant competition authorities.

7.4.7 Unfair commercial practices

Another legal issue that has been widely debated is the issue of what constitutes unfair trade practices. The European Commission conducted an exploration of issues concerning companies' trust in what the Commission chose to call Internet Trading Platforms (ITPs). The reason behind this work was that many manufacturing companies experienced problems with the new buying technologies, and felt that these technologies did little else than pressure prices. SMEs also felt that the technological integration was burdensome to them.[35] In particular, the use of reverse auctions was felt to be questionable and unfair to companies.[36] The Expert Group set up by the Commission id however not recommend any new laws to deal with the anxiety felt by SMEs. Instead, *codes of conduct* were recommended to solve outstanding issues and problems. The Expert Group also outlined some general guidelines containing recommendations on what such a code could contain.[37]

7.4.8 Public procurement law

In the special case where the procurement we are studying is public procurement, a whole new set of laws and rules are applicable to the procedures. We shall examine the Swedish law on this matter to give a few examples of issues that have to be raised.

---

35 Report of the Expert Group on B2B Internet trading platforms (Final report), pp. 11–12,
http://www.europa.eu.int/comm/enterprise/ict/policy/b2b/wshop/fin-report.pdf.
36 Report of the Expert Group on B2B Internet trading platforms (Final report), p. 17,
http://www.europa.eu.int/comm/enterprise/ict/policy/b2b/wshop/fin-report.pdf.
37 The group did *not* outline a code of conduct of its own, but rather listed a number of possible conditions that such a code could contain.

The Public Procurement Act (SFS 1992:1528) regulates public procurement in Sweden. The portal paragraph in the law states simply that:[38]

> The award of public contracts should be so arranged as to take advantage of existing competition and should also in other respects accord with the conventions of good business practice. No unwarranted considerations should affect the treatment of tenderers, candidates or tenders.

This first provision also offers a challenge to electronic public procurement. One possible line of argument would be this: requiring companies to use electronic procurement (and only electronic procurement) cannot be allowed under the act, since the mode of communication cannot be relevant to the award of the contract. If a contracting entity were to require certain modes of communication the potential sellers should be able to challenge that requirement under the law.

Is this a sound argument? That is hard to say, but the answer is probably yes. There are two possible answers, however, that allow the use of e-procurement all the same.

The first is that the entire problem can be eliminated if the contracting entity assumes the cost of the communication. If the contracting entity simply states that "the procurement process will be conducted online and all who do not have the available means to participate, but wish to do so, will be given those means by us" it seems likely that there would be little to complain about.

The second answer is that a contracting entity may of course use multiple channels of communication with the sellers or bidders. This would probably be the general reply if someone complained that the process was conducted online: to ensure that conventional bids were also possible and not discriminated against.[39]

When studying procurement law and electronic procurement we generally find at least two kinds of problems:

---

38 Chapter 1 section 4.
39 One way of encouraging e-procurement would be to give extra points when evaluating bids to those that used the electronic procurement system. Under today's Act this would probably not be allowed.

1 Problems of interpreting the law's requirements in a legal environment (*translation problems*). These are problems arising out of the conceptual framework that the law works with, and the general off-line reference framework that the law was conceived within. How to translate off-line behaviours to on-line practices is the essential issue in these problems.

2 Problems of introducing new procurement methods (*introduction problems*). One example of this is the problem that we touched briefly on above. Is it unwarranted to introduce electronic processes in the procurement situation? Here the issue is not one of translation as much as one of general applicability. Can the law at all be fulfilled with different methods and technologies than the ones used at the time the law was written?

The first category is often difficult. To illustrate this we can study one section of the act that deals with the rights of sellers to ensure that the bids are opened and treated equally. The act clearly specifies such a right in Chapter 1 Section 20:

> **20 §** Envelopes containing tenders are to be opened as soon as possible after the final date for receipt of tenders in the presence of at least two individuals appointed by the contracting entity. A written record of tenders shall be drawn up, and the accuracy of this record shall be confirmed by those participating in the opening. Should a tenderer so request, an individual appointed by a Chamber of Commerce shall also be present, the cost to be defrayed by the tenderer making the request.
>
> When negotiated procedures (förhandlad upphandling) are used, the tenders may be opened and recorded without the formalities enjoined in the preceding paragraph. The tenders shall be opened simultaneously or, if there are particular grounds for doing so, one by one as they are received.

Note the provision that states that a tenderer can request to have an individual appointed by a Chamber of Commerce present during the opening of tenders. How can this right be translated to the electronic world? Several different alternatives present themselves. Firstly, it is arguable that this rule cannot apply in electronic procurement, and that the right thus can no longer be guaranteed. This would mean that tenderers suffer a loss of rights when we move to the new medium. Why this would be appropriate is less than clear, and we should not accept translations where rights previously granted are simply eliminated. Secondly, we may argue that there is an electronic process such that it is equal to the process described in the paragraph above. This is exactly what chambers have argued. By developing special e-procurement services Chambers of Commerce in Sweden have developed an electronic procedure that is a translation of the right to have an appointed official examine the opening of tenders. This method – e-anbud – simply works as an electronic notariat that identifies the officials opening the tenders, the tenders and then creates a log file showing that the tenders have each been opened.[40] This attitude calls for what can be termed an *equivalence of rights*, that is: changing the mode of procuring should not change the rights of the parties involved. A third possible answer is to argue that the shift to electronic services should be utilised to *strengthen* the rights set out in the act. Why only monitor the opening of the tenders, when we can monitor the entire internal process of evaluating, deciding and contracting? This view represents a form of business process re-engineering perspective, and seems to encourage what we could term technology-made or enhanced rights. A fourth answer would be to re-write the act in order to adapt it to new technologies. This updating attitude may end up either strengthening or weakening the rights of the participants according to new political sentiments.

Is e-procurement possible today, then, without changes in the act? The answer to that seems to be a tentative "yes". The main requirements, according to procurement experts[41], are that the bids must not be available to the contracting entity before the end of the tendering period (secrecy requirement), the technology used may not be complicated or expensive or otherwise discriminate against small and medium-sized companies or other categories of tenderers (technology discrimination requirement), exact time and date for the submission and reception of tenders must be determinable (the time requirement) and access to tenders must be restricted to authorised and identifiable individuals at legitimate times (the authorisation requirement).

---

40 *See* http://www.e-anbud.se.
41 *See* http://www.nou.se/pdf/konf_foredrag/Seminarium4.pdf.

If these requirements are met, it seems likely that electronic public procurement would meet with no legal objections. Several Swedish municipalities are experimenting with full scale e-procurement with good success.[42]

7.5 Public procurement principles and e-procurement

7.5.1 Introduction

The European legal framework for public procurement partly builds on a number of principles. It is illuminating to examine these, and to reason about how they are connected with electronic public procurement. Reading the principles also give an overview of the important general conditions that electronic procurement has to fulfil in the public procurement case. The principles are available in many different versions. The one used here has been published in an overview of Swedish legislation, and can be considered as fairly common to the EU member states.[43]

7.5.2 Principle of non-discrimination

Let us begin with the principle of non-discrimination:

> The principle of non-discrimination prohibits all discrimination based on nationality. No contracting entity may, for example, give preference to a local company simply because it is located in the municipality.

This is fairly straight-forward, and the applicability to e-procurement may seem far-fetched. But there are interesting hypothetical cases here. What if local companies have the electronic means to participate, but companies in other member states in the European Union do not? Would that mean that the use of electronic public procurement violated the principle of non-discrimination?

---

42 *See* http://www.chambersign.se/docs/E-signweb.pdf.
43 *A brief description of LOU, the Public Procurement Act, and NOU, the National Board for Public Procurement*, p. 4,. http://www.nou.se/pdf/english.pdf.

Perhaps. At least it seems arguable that the contracting entity should be responsible for supplying all tenderers with relevant technology, or accept and not discriminate against, tenders that are delivered by traditional means.

7.5.3 Principle of equal treatment

The principle of equal treatment states that:[44]

> [...] all suppliers must be treated equally. All suppliers involved in a procurement procedure must, for example, be given the same information at the same time.

This is an intriguing principle, and one that seems to have at least some relevance to the design of e-procurement platforms. Information dissemination within these platforms should then be design as to ensure that information reaches all suppliers at the same time. This can be done by time-stamping information as it is sent out, but all that would prove is when it was sent. If we also want to ensure that it is available at the same time, it seems better to make it accessible centrally at a certain time rather than "push" it to the suppliers.

7.5.4 Principle of transparency

This principle states that:[45]

> [...] the procurement process must be characterised by predictability and openness. In order to ensure equal conditions for tenderers the contract document has to be clear and unambiguous and contain all the requirements made of the items to be procured.

This seems less relevant to electronic procurement. One possibility is to argue that the principle implies that the contract document must be made available in a format that is sure not to leave something out if it is used with a different version of the word processing software than the one in which it was written. That does not seem likely.

---

44 *A brief description of LOU, the Public Procurement Act, and NOU, the National Board for Public Procurement,* p. 4, http://www.nou.se/pdf/english.pdf.

45 *A brief description of LOU, the Public Procurement Act, and NOU, the National Board for Public Procurement,* p. 4, http://www.nou.se/pdf/english.pdf.

7.5.5   Principle of proportionality

The principle of proportionality states that:[46]

> [...] qualification requirements and requirements regarding the subject matter of the contract must have a natural relation to the supplies, services or works which are being procured and not be disproportionate.

Again not particularly relevant to electronic procurement.

7.5.6   Principle of mutual recognition

The principle of mutual recognition simply states that:

> [...] documents and certificates issued by the appropriate authorities in a Member State must be accepted in the other Member States.

Here the relevance may be higher. What about electronic certificates and signatures? Should the security technology applied in one country be accepted in all others? Should the contracting entity be forced to adapt to signature and security schemes in all member states? This would surely be an absurd over-interpretation of the general principle. What remains relevant to ask is whether this means that the systems need to be tailored to ensure interoperability with different document standards and certification practices (not necessarily in the sense "electronic certificates") in other member states.

7.5.7   Conclusions

The principles of public procurement seem to allow for electronic procurement, but with the same general caveat as the one introduced above: technology must not be used in a discriminatory way or in a way that unduly excludes certain categories of companies from competition.

---

46   *A brief description of LOU, the Public Procurement Act, and NOU, the National Board for Public Procurement*, p. 4, http://www.nou.se/pdf/english.pdf.

7.6   Some practical issues

7.6.1   Codes of conduct

The development of e-procurement platforms, e-markets and similar systems is now the focus of considerable legal and political interest. This has led to the development of several different codes of conduct, self-regulatory tools that can be used to clarify at least some of the more difficult issues surrounding these systems. [47]

7.6.2   Price mechanisms – especially auctions

One of the main problems with e-procurement of different kinds has been the choice of price mechanisms. Auctions especially seem to have generated much interest and political debate. There are numerous different auction forms and the legal framework for auctions is far from set.

7.7   Some notes on the on-going revision of procurement law

In the European Union a new legislative package has been adopted to modernise public procurement.[48] This has been followed up by an action plan on e-procurement from the European Commission.[49] The revision will open up entirely new possibilities if all the possibilities offered in the legislative package are implemented by

---

47   See for an overview Communication from the Commission to the Council, the European Parliament and the European Economic and Social Committee, *Enhancing Trust and Confidence in Business-to-Business Electronic Markets,* COM (2004) 479 final.

48   Primarily in Directive 2004/17/EC of the European Parliament and of the Council of 31 March 2004 coordinating the procurement procedures of entities operating in the water, energy, transport and postal services sectors (30.04.2004) and Directive 2004/18/EC of the European Parliament and of the Council of 31 March 2004 on the coordination of procedures for the award of public works contracts, public supply contracts and public service contracts (30.04.2004).

49   *See* http://europa.eu.int/comm/internal_market/publicprocurement/e-procurement_en.htm#actionplan.

the Member States. Among the changes is found a new form of procurement: dynamic purchasing systems (Article 1 p. 6).[50] This new form is defined as a system that is "a completely electronic process for making commonly used purchases, the characteristics of which, as generally available on the market, meet the requirements of the contracting authority, which is limited in duration and open throughout its validity to any economic operator which satisfies the selection criteria and has submitted an indicative tender that complies with the specification.".

The new form is regulated in detail in Article 33 Directive 2004/18/EC.

Dynamic purchasing systems

1 Member States may provide that contracting authorities may use dynamic purchasing systems.

It is noteworthy that the legislative package does not mandate the introduction of this new form of procurement procedure.

The actual process of setting up a system is described in some detail:

2 In order to set up a dynamic purchasing system, contracting authorities shall follow the rules of the open procedure in all its phases up to the award of the contracts to be concluded under this system. All the tenderers satisfying the selection criteria and having submitted an indicative tender which complies with the specification and any possible additional documents shall be admitted to the system; indicative tenders may be improved at any time provided that they continue to comply with the specification. With a view to setting up the system and to the award of contracts under that system, contracting authorities shall use solely electronic means in accordance with Article 42(2) to (5).

Here the directive mandates the use of "electronic means". This is defined in the directive as "using electronic equipment for the processing (including digital compression) and storage of data which is transmitted, conveyed and received by wire, by radio, by optical means or by other electromagnetic means." The relevant Ar-

---

50 Definitions from Directive 2004/18/EC Article 1.

ticles referenced are set up to eliminate the risk that the means for communication are exclusionary or discriminatory.[51]

A dynamic purchasing system can only be used if it is well specified and published:

> 3 For the purposes of setting up the dynamic purchasing system, contracting authorities shall:
>
> (a) publish a contract notice making it clear that a dynamic purchasing system is involved;
>
> (b) indicate in the specification, amongst other matters, the nature of the purchases envisaged under that system, as well as all the necessary information concerning the purchasing system, the electronic equipment used and the technical connection arrangements and specifications;
>
> (c) offer by electronic means, on publication of the notice and up to the expiry of the system, unrestricted, direct and full access to the specification and to any additional documents and shall indicate in the notice the internet address at which such documents may be consulted.

---

51 The requirements are: "2. The means of communication chosen must be generally available and thus not restrict economic operators' access to the tendering procedure. 3. Communication and the exchange and storage of information shall be carried out in such a way as to ensure that the integrity of data and the confidentiality of tenders and requests to participate are preserved, and that the contracting authorities examine the content of tenders and requests to participate only after the time limit set for submitting them has expired. 4. The tools to be used for communicating by electronic means, as well as their technical characteristics, must be non-discriminatory, generally available and interoperable with the information and communication technology products in general use.
5. The following rules are applicable to devices for the electronic transmission and receipt of tenders and to devices for the electronic receipt of requests to participate: (a) information regarding the specifications necessary for the electronic submission of tenders and requests to participate, including encryption, shall be available to interested parties. Moreover, the devices for the electronic receipt of tenders and requests to participate shall conform to the requirements of Annex X; (b) Member States may, in compliance with Article 5 of Directive 1999/93/EC, require that electronic tenders be accompanied by an advanced electronic signature in conformity with paragraph 1 thereof;
(c) Member States may introduce or maintain voluntary accreditation schemes aiming at enhanced levels of certification service provision for these devices; (d) tenderers or candidates shall undertake to submit, before expiry of the time limit laid down for submission of tenders or requests to participate, the documents, certificates and declarations referred to in Articles 45 to 50 and Article 52 if they do not exist in electronic format."

And it is important that the systems be non-exclusionary, and that all tenders be evaluated.

> 4 Contracting authorities shall give any economic operator, through-out the entire period of the dynamic purchasing system, the possi-bility of submitting an indicative tender and of being admitted to the system under the conditions referred to in paragraph 2. They shall complete evaluation within a maximum of 15 days from the date of submission of the indicative tender. However, they may ex-tend the evaluation period provided that no invitation to tender is issued in the meantime.
> The contracting authority shall inform the tenderer referred to in the first subparagraph at the earliest possible opportunity of its ad-mittance to the dynamic purchasing system or of the rejection of its indicative tender.

This means that we find a *two-tier system* in the Directive: first an in-dicative tender is submitted, and the bidder is admitted to the sys-tem. This can be read as a qualification procedure that may also be used to eliminate simple mistakes from inexperienced bidders. This also leads to a two-tier publishing procedure:

> 5 Each specific contract must be the subject of an invitation to ten-der. Before issuing the invitation to tender, contracting authorities shall publish a simplified contract notice inviting all interested economic operators to submit an indicative tender, in accordance with paragraph 4, within a time limit that may not be less than 15 days from the date on which the simplified notice was sent. Con-tracting authorities may not proceed with tendering until they have completed evaluation of all the indicative tenders received by that deadline.

Regular procurement principles apply:

> 6 Contracting authorities shall invite all tenderers admitted to the system to submit a tender for each specific contract to be awarded under the system. To that end they shall set a time limit for the submission of tenders.
>
> They shall award the contract to the tenderer which submitted the best tender on the basis of the award criteria set out in the contract notice for the establishment of the dynamic purchasing system. Those criteria may, if appropriate, be formulated more precisely in the invitation referred to in the first subparagraph.

In order to ensure that these systems do not coagulate into cartels or any other form of collusion, the directive specifies a time limit. The legislative package also clearly states that no charges may be used for these systems: this would risk violating the non-discrimination principles. Especially if these fees were very high:

> 7 A dynamic purchasing system may not last for more than four years, except in duly justified exceptional cases.
>
> Contracting authorities may not resort to this system to prevent, restrict or distort competition.
>
> No charges may be billed to the interested economic operators or to parties to the system.

The legislative package also opens up the possibility of using electronic auctions in public procurement, as a new price mechanism. An electronic auction is defined (Article 1 p. 7) as "a repetitive process involving an electronic device for the presentation of new prices, revised downwards, and/or new values concerning certain elements of tenders, which occurs after an initial full evaluation of the tenders, enabling them to be ranked using automatic evaluation methods." This also implies that some objects cannot be procured this way (Art. 6 p. 7): "Consequently, certain service contracts and certain works contracts having as their subject-matter intellectual performances, such as the design of works, may not be the object of electronic auctions.".

Public electronic procurement is – in the legislative packages – subject to different security requirements. As we have seen above, there is a requirement of integrity and authenticity, akin to the one found in e-invoicing legislation in the European Union.[52] In more detail we find in Annex X:

> Devices for the electronic receipt of tenders, requests for participation and plans and projects in contests must at least guarantee, through technical means and appropriate procedures, that:
>
> (a) electronic signatures relating to tenders, requests to participate and the forwarding of plans and projects comply with national provisions adopted pursuant to Directive 1999/93/EC;

---

52 *See* Council Directive 2001/115/EC of 20 December 2001 amending Directive 77/388/EEC with a view to simplifying, modernising and harmonising the conditions laid down for invoicing in respect of value added tax.

147

(b) the exact time and date of the receipt of tenders, requests to participate and the submission of plans and projects can be determined precisely;

(c) it may be reasonably ensured that, before the time limits laid down, no-one can have access to data transmitted under these requirements;

(d) if that access prohibition is infringed, it may be reasonably ensured that the infringement is clearly detectable;

(e) only authorised persons may set or change the dates for opening data received;

(f) during the different stages of the contract award procedure or of the contest access to all data submitted, or to part thereof, must be possible only through simultaneous action by authorised persons;

(g) simultaneous action by authorised persons must give access to data transmitted only after the prescribed date;

(h) data received and opened in accordance with these requirements must remain accessible only to persons authorised to acquaint themselves therewith.

That these requirements have direct impact on system design is clearly obvious. In order to ensure compliance with this legislation systems being built today should of course take the legislative package into account.

7.8 Concluding remarks

Electronic procurement is a difficult area, and the design of electronic procurement platforms is a project that involves both technical and legal complexities. It is important that these complexities are dealt with simultaneously as to ensure that the end result is not a technical situation that is legally controversial, or indeed a legal situation that is impossible to implement in a technical architecture. This chapter has attempted to show some of the often very practical legal problems that face the developer of e-procurement platforms. It seems fair to say that e-procurement is a field that presents complex techno-legal problems and that as such it is well suited for further study.

8 Electronic signatures in a legal context

Anna Nordén

8.1 Terminology

8.1.1 The signature concept

A signature can generally be defined as a mark meant to tie information to the person making it. This tie is often described in terms of *authenticity, integrity* and *non-repudiation*.[1] A signature should indicate who signed the message and it should ideally be difficult for another person to reproduce that signature. This assurance that data originates from its purported source is normally referred to as *authenticity*.[2] A signature should further identify what is signed. In an ideal world, this identification should make it difficult to alter the data without detection. This *integrity* function can be defined as assurance that data has not been changed after it was signed. The authenticity and the integrity of information are important functions of what is called *non-repudiation,* which is often technically defined as assurance against false denial of the message by the signer.[3] It should be noted that these functions are not always equally well achieved – e.g. in the paper environment the paper as such is a vital component in addition to the signature to achieve integrity. In the

---

1 It should be noted that not all signatures, on paper or electronic, can achieve those functions to the same extent.

2 Technically this function is also referred to as *data origin authentication* and should be distinguished from *peer entity authentication; see further* European Committee for Standardization (CEN), Guide on the Use of Electronic Signatures – Part 1: Legal and Technical Aspects, CEN Workshop Agreement 14365, Ref. No CWA 14365-1:2004 E pp. 9.

3 *See* American Bar Association (ABA), *Digital Signature Guidelines (with comments),* 1996 http://www.abanet.org/scitech/ec/isc/dsgfree.html, pp. 8–9, Udsen, Henrik, *Den digitale signatur – ansvarsspörgsmål*, Forlaget Thomson A/S, Copenhagen, 2002, p. 17. *See further* CEN Workshop Agreement CWA 14365-1:2004 pp. 9. In the ISO standards this aspect is referred to as "non-repudiation of origin". For more on technical vs. legal aspects of non-repudiation, *see* 9.4.4 below.

electronic world, too, some "signatures" are better or worse that others at achieving these signature aims.

It should be remembered that for most common legal purposes, a signature is not a hard requirement. Just as an ink signature is seldom required for most paper contracts to be valid, so an electronic contract or other legal act seldom needs to be signed with an electronic signature. However, in order to be able to prove what has been agreed to and by whom, contracts are often signed for evidence's sake.

Before the information technology age the concept of signature was equal to the manual (handwritten) signature. As a result of digitisation a need emerged for a mechanism that could ensure the integrity and authenticity of the digital document and its contents. Since the digital document in many cases replaces the paper document, it is not surprising that the paper world was used as the basis for terminology – thus the word "signature" was used for the methods to ensure the same functionalities as the handwritten signature had done in the paper world. The word electronic signature is thus the common terminology for methods used to replace the handwritten signature. However, it needs to be kept in mind that there are significant differences between handwritten signatures and electronic signatures, and so the paper analogy is not always correct.[4]

8.1.2 The legal notion of electronic signatures

In a legal context, "electronic signature" is a generic, technology-neutral term signifying all methods by which one can "legally sign" electronic data. It aims to replace the legal signature (often handwritten) of the paper world – "the signer signs a contract".[5] An elec-

---

4   *See e.g.* Bryde Andersen, Mads, *IT-retten*, First edition, Forlaget IT-retten, Copenhagen, 2001, p. 746. For a comprehensive analysis of the functions of and a comparison between manual and electronic signatures see CEN Workshop Agreement CWA 14365-1:2004, pp. 12–13.

5   The notion of "signature" as it is used in Directive 1999/93/EC of the European Parliament and of the Council of 13 December 1999 on a Community framework for electronic signatures, ("E-Signature Directive") refers to a legal and not to a technical concept. Jos Dumortier et al., *The Legal and Market Aspects of Electronic Signatures*, Study for the European Commission – DG Information Society, Service Contract No C 28.400, Leuven: Interdisciplinary centre for Law and Information Technology, 2003, p. 29.

tronic signature can take many forms and can be created by many different technologies. It is thus not specific to any type of technology, e.g. a digital signature enabled by PKI (Public Key Infrastructure, see further PKI technology below). Rather, the definition of electronic signature varies from one law to another, ranging from very wide methods of authentication, such as a name typed by the sender at the end of the e-mail, a digitised image of a handwritten signature attached to an electronic document, to digital signatures based on PKI technology.

8.1.3 Digital vs. electronic signatures

To many people, in particular those with a technical background, the electronic signature is synonymous to a digital signature. This is not necessarily the case in the lawyer's world. Rather, the concept of electronic signature includes digital signatures, as well as many other means to "sign electronically". Electronic signature is thus more broadly defined than digital signature. In figure 8.1 this is visualised using examples of what may legally constitute electronic signatures; however it should be noted that the definition varies among laws. The figure is thus not representative of all e-signature laws; some laws even restrict the definition of electronic signatures to digital signatures only.

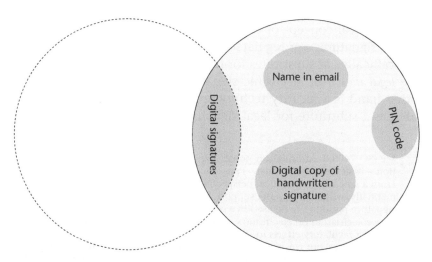

Figure 8.1 The legal notion of electronic signatures.

From e legal perspective a digital signature is often defined as an electronic signature based on a specific technical solution (PKI). A digital signature can also be based on other technologies,[6] but since PKI is the predominant technology the terms "digital signature" and "PKI-based signature" are normally used interchangeably, which is also the case in this chapter.[7] PKI can in addition to be used for digital signatures also provide confidentiality of data.

In many cases the term electronic signature is used when the "correct" more specific terminology would be digital signature. One reason for this is that the digital signature is the only viable option today to reach the level of integrity, authenticity and non-repudiation that is required for many common purposes in digital environments. Further, most laws in the area have chosen the wider term electronic signature, even when the legislator had digital signatures in mind.[8] The purported rationale of using broader terminology than justified by the actual focus of such laws is to make the regulations more technology-neutral and hopefully more future-proof.[9] For many people "electronic signature" has thus in practice come to mean "digital signature".

8.1.4 The legal notion vs. the technical concept

Very often electronic signatures or digital signatures are discussed without giving any thought as to whether it is the legal notion or the technical concept of the signature that is meant. When electronic signatures are regulated in e-signature laws the definition typically aims at substitutes for legal signatures (here referred to as *the legal notion* of electronic signatures). Digital signature on the other hand is a security technology based on PKI – which *can* be used as a substitute for legal signatures, but is often also used for

---

6   See ISO 7498-2: Information processing systems – Open Systems Interconnection – Basic Reference Model – Part 2: Security Architecture, 1989.
7   From a strictly mathematical perspective a digital signature could be computed manually, without computer support. In the digital society, however, the digital signature presumes to be used in a computer context.
8   *See e.g.* legislation on electronic signatures in the EU and by UNCITRAL.
9   The first regulatory efforts in the area in the mid 90s specifically addressed digital signatures, but this was heavily criticised for being too technology-specific. Work on the E-Signature Directive also used the term "digital signatures" in the early days.

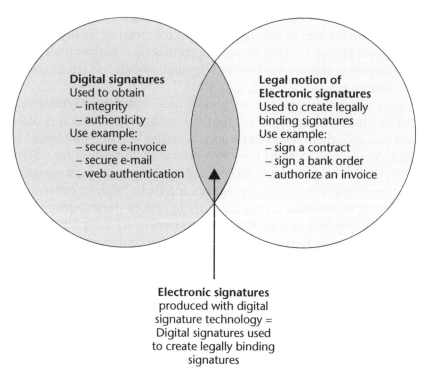

Digital signatures
Used to obtain
– integrity
– authenticity
Use example:
– secure e-invoice
– secure e-mail
– web authentication

Legal notion of Electronic signatures
Used to create legally
binding signatures
Use example:
– sign a contract
– sign a bank order
– authorize an invoice

Electronic signatures
produced with digital
signature technology =
Digital signatures used
to create legally binding
signatures

Figure 8.2 The legal notion vs the technical concept of electronic signatures.

other purposes. This may be anything from ensuring the integrity and authenticity of an electronic invoice or e-mail to authentication towards a web-portal. (See figure 8.2.)

It should be noted that the fact that an application uses digital signatures for other reasons than to create legally binding signatures, does not mean that there are no legal considerations involved. The legal and policy aspects of PKI (see sections Policies and procedures in a PKI and Legal aspects of electronic signatures below) are still applicable, and in many cases digital signatures are used for traceability purposes, i.e. to prove what communication or transaction took place and at what time. Legal considerations may also be requirements in law for integrity and authenticity – still without aim to replace legal signatures.

The distinction between the legal and the technical concepts is important when implementing electronic signatures; an application may e.g. use digital signatures for both entity authentication (e.g. access control to a web portal) and for creating legally binding electronic signatures (e.g. in signing contracts).[10] Unfortunately the distinction is not always properly upheld, which has led to confusion among both users and legislators.[11]

One important aspect of using electronic signatures to create substitutes for legal signatures is that the technology as such is often not enough; there needs to be an affirmative act, an "intention" to sign. Many legal systems have this notion of "intention (or intent) to be bound" as a criterion for concluding a contract.[12] If a signature has been placed without the signer's intent to "sign in order to be bound by the contract", but e.g. only to ensure the integrity of the message, this will not be sufficient to constitute a legally binding contract. The problem in the electronic environment is that it is often less clear than in the paper environment whether a signature conveys intent to be bound since the same "signature" is used both for signing contracts and as a mere security technology. Further, there is no tradition of using electronic signatures for contract signing in the way that there is with ink signatures.[13] Handwritten signatures always require some concentration on the part of the signer whereas an electronic signature can be placed with only a minimum

10 The Legal and Market Aspects of Electronic Signatures, pp. 29–30.
11 One example is the EU VAT directive harmonising electronic invoicing (Council Directive 2001/115/EC amending Directive 77/388/EEC with a view to simplifying, modernising and harmonising the conditions laid down for invoicing in respect of value added tax), which includes requirements for "advanced electronic signatures" to ensure integrity and authenticity from a technical perspective – i.e. not with the purpose of replacing handwritten signatures. Many EU member states have implemented these requirements as legal signature-equivalents to handwritten signatures, which has led to laws that are inconsistent with the technical use of digital signatures. See further International Chamber of Commerce (ICC), *ICC comment on the use of advanced electronic signatures by legal persons for security purposes*, March 2003, Commission on E-Business, IT and Telecoms Task Force on Security and Authentication, Doc 373-36/4, Paris, 2003.
12 Certain laws include the "intention" factor already as a part of the legal e-signature definition, e.g. the UNCITRAL Model Law on Electronic Signatures, the US e-commerce legislation.
13 *See* Udsen, Henrik, *Den digitale signatur – ansvarsspörgsmål*, pp. 55 on the issue of whether a digital signature as such can be seen as a manifestation of will. It has also been discussed what legal relevance a technical setting of "key usage" in the certificate to "non-repudiation" has – would it imply "intent to be bound"? Depending on the policy governing the certificate it could have some relevance, but it is very unlikely that a judge would find this fact alone of decisive importance.

of voluntary involvement of the signer. For this reason it is particularly important that the "intent" be ensured and considered in the system design. The design of the user interface is one way to replicate the "ceremonial" aspect of a handwritten signature, thus ensuring that the electronic signature include a manifestation of will.[14]

Thus, no single implementation of electronic signatures – whether for pure technical security purposes or to obtain a legal effect – can be meaningful without considering all relevant aspects: a system development approach is needed that in addition to technical and legal aspects takes account of organisational issues, as well as matters such as application area and sector of use.[15]

To summarise the distinctions between an electronic and a digital signature, and the legal notion and the technical concept of signatures,

- the legal notion of an electronic signature includes anything that is used to *replace the legal signature* of the paper world; the exact definition varies among laws;
- digital signature is just *one* kind of electronic signature;
- digital signature is a security technology, which may be used for different purposes, e.g.
  - *replace the legal signature*, e.g. when signing a contract (in which case it is an electronic signature from a legal perspective);
  - to provide *integrity* and *authenticity* of data, e.g. when securing an electronic invoice.
- PKI, the technology on which the digital signature is based, can further be used to provide *confidentiality* of data, e.g. when sending an e-mail or other business communication.

8.1.5 Legal focus on digital signatures and PKI

The digital signature based on PKI is the predominant electronic signature technology used today to achieve authenticity, control of in-

---

14 SAMSET (Samhällets elektroniska tjänster) is a Swedish initiative within the area of e-supported public services, http://www.rsv.se/samset/samset/html, where an aim is to make the user aware of what he or she signs and why.
15 For an analysis of practical issues of e-signatures from a legal point of view and challenges in the context of implementation see Magnusson Sjöberg, Cecilia, Nordén, Anna, *Managing Electronic Signatures – Current Challenges,* in Wahlgren, Peter (ed.), *IT Law,* Scandinavian Studies in Law, vol. 47, Stockholm Institute for Scandinavian Law, 2004, pp. 79–98.

tegrity, and non-repudiation. Further, in all e-signature legislation, digital signatures are the only area where the aim of the regulation goes further than just creating equivalence between handwritten and other signatures. Digital signature-specific rules laid down in electronic signature laws often deal with liability aspects and sometimes also with other PKI-specific issues such as certification and supervision. For these reasons digital signatures and PKI have many interesting legal aspects, which is why this chapter emphasises digital signatures and the PKI-technology in a legal context.

Many people, in particular those with a technical background, tend to think of digital signatures as a purely technical method of achieving data security. The legal aspects are very often forgotten or taken for granted. In fact, it was only in the beginning of the 90s that lawyers started paying attention to PKI. However, the full trust-enhancing potential of PKI can only be realised through a proper interplay between technological, policy and legal components. Without a rules infrastructure governing the PKI it will be very difficult for parties in electronic transactions to achieve an acceptable level of legal certainty. For the last decade, therefore, a *legal framework* has been developing directed towards acceptance of legal use of electronic signatures in general and digital signatures in particular.

8.2   PKI technology[16]

8.2.1   Public key cryptography

PKI is based on a technology called *public key cryptography,* which in turn is based on *algorithms* and *keys.* A cryptographic algorithm is a set of steps for rendering plain information unintelligible (*encryption*), and for restoring encrypted information to intelligible form (*decryption*). Encryption and decryption are performed with cryptographic *keys.* Keys are parameters that are input to a particular cryptographic algorithm to fully specify how it should process an input.

---

16   This chapter as well as chapters 9.3 and 9.4 are to a large extent based on Trust-Weaver AB's white papers "PKI Technology Basics" and "Legal aspects of PKI", published on http://www.trustweaver.com. For a deeper understanding of the technology see e.g. Schneier, Bruce, *Applied Cryptography – Protocols, Algorithms, and Source Code in C,* John Wiley & Sons, Inc., New York, 1996.

Keys can have different lengths, measured in bits. Longer keys are more secure than short keys provided that the algorithm itself is secure.

There are two types of cryptographic algorithms: secret key and public key.

Secret key (or *symmetric*) algorithms use one and the same key for encryption and decryption. The principal disadvantage of secret key algorithms is that users have to agree on a key before a secure connection can be established. This feature also means that secret key algorithms are not suitable for obtaining non-repudiation functions. However since this method is fast it is often used in combination with public key encryption (see below). The most commonly used secret key algorithms include *DES, AES, RC4 and IDEA.*

Public key (or *asymmetric*) encryption uses two keys that mathematically correspond to one another in such a way that information encrypted with key A can be decrypted only with key B. However, the keys cannot be derived from one another. This attribute is used in public key cryptography by calling key A the *private key* and key B the *public key.* As their names indicate, the public key can be published freely while the private key must be kept secret. Anyone can use a public key to encrypt information for a specific recipient. Only the holder of the private key can decrypt the information. The main benefit of public key encryption is that this allows people who have no pre-existing security arrangement to exchange information securely. The disadvantage of this technique is that most public key encryption algorithms are comparatively slow and thus not suited to encrypt large messages. The most commonly used public key algorithm is *RSA.*

Most of today's security protocols use a combination of public key and secret key encryption. This typically means that public key algorithms are used to securely exchange a secret key ("session key"), which is then used to encrypt the actual data with a secret key algorithm.

8.2.2   Digital Signatures

Public key algorithms can do something that is not achievable with secret key algorithms: they can be used to create *digital signatures.* The first step in digitally signing a message is to produce a unique thumbprint, a *hash*, of the message. A hash is a fixed-size number from which the original message cannot be re-constituted. Well-known cryptographic hash functions are *MD5* (Message Digest Algorithm 5) and *SHA* (Secure Hash Algorithm). The hash is then encrypted using the private key and attached to the original message. The recipient will decrypt the hash using the sender's public key, re-compute the hash on the message and compare the two hashes. If they match, the recipient can be certain of both the identity of the sender's private key and the integrity of the message.

RSA and DSA are algorithms used for digital signing.

8.2.3 From public key cryptography to Public Key Infrastructure (PKI)

While the techniques described above can provide a high degree of technical certainty, they do not provide a way to associate public keys to specific individuals or entities. Thus, their practical value is rather limited. After all, what good is it to know that I can encrypt a message if I cannot be sure that I am restricting the ability to decrypt to the right party? Similarly, a digital signature does not have a great practical value if I have no way to establish the identity of the signer.

When using public key algorithms for digital signatures and key exchange it is vital to be sure that a public key (and thus the private key) belongs to an identified person or entity. In small or functionally limited communities, users can agree on a process that allows keys to be used with a high degree of trust. However, in larger or more complex groups such trust is easily undermined due to the difficulties inherent in managing large numbers of keys.

PKI solves this problem by creating a technically verifiable association between a public key and a specific individual or entity. This association is established through a *digital certificate*. Today's global technical standard for digital certificates is x.509v3.

Digital signatures based on PKI thus supports authenticity in addition to control of data integrity.[17]

---

17 Digital signatures in themselves do not achieve data integrity; rather they offer the possibility to control that data hasn't changed. (Digital signatures also do not produce confidentiality, although a PKI implementation gives encryption possibilities.)

8.2.4 Players in a PKI

8.2.4.1 Certification Authority

The technically verifiable association between a public key and a specific individual or entity in a PKI is established through a digital certificate. The entity issuing the certificate and thus vouching for the link to the user is called Certification Authority (CA) and is the hub of a PKI.

A certificate, containing the public key as well as information concerning the identity of the holder of the corresponding private key, is in turn digitally signed by the CA. This creates a potential for establishing a more centralised (and thus more easily manageable) security model, if the CA can be trusted by all other players. By signing a certificate, the CA sends the message that the certificate is trustworthy.

In addition to registering and identifying users and issue certificates to them, the CA can also revoke certificates that have been issued. Revocation normally occurs when a private key has been compromised, or when the data in a certificate has changed and is no longer correct. If a certificate is revoked, the CA must make this information available to prevent other parties from relying on this certificate. This is traditionally done by publishing a CRL (Certificate Revocation List), which contains the revoked (and thus unreliable) certificates. This mechanism can be complemented or replaced by more modern protocols such as OCSP (On-line Certificate Status Protocol) and XKMSValidate (XML Key Management Specification validation protocol).

To the CA functions should be added lifecycle management of certificates, which regulates procedures, e.g. for expiry and renewal of certificates and keys.

The CA is sometimes also referred to as the "issuer" or the "trusted third party", although the latter may have a somewhat different meaning (see Trusted Third Parties below). The term Certification Service Provider ("CSP")[18] is also used, which is often intended to include a wider range of services than the traditional certification

---

18 Not to be confused with Cryptographic Service Provider.

service, such as e.g. time-stamping. The actual identification and registration process can be carried out by a separate entity normally referred to as a Registration Authority (RA).

8.2.4.2 Certificate holder

The certificate holder is the natural or legal person to whom a certificate is issued, and who is identified in the certificate. One point deserving attention is that certificates "issued" to IT resources (an e-mail address, a server etc) are legally speaking always issued to a natural or legal person, because an IT resource cannot in itself hold rights and obligations.

Before the certificate holder receives the certificate the CA normally requires it to enter into an agreement, taking on certain obligations with respect to the certificate and keys. The certificate holder's most important obligations are to keep its private key strictly for itself (protect it against compromise), and to immediately notify the CA if it knows of or suspects such compromise. These obligations are often referred to as "certificate holder obligations".

A certificate holder can also be referred to as "key holder", "end entity", "user", "subscriber", "signatory" or "signer".

8.2.4.3 Relying party

A relying party is someone who relies on a signature that has been created using the private key and the corresponding certificate. Before acting on a signature the relying party needs to verify that the underlying certificate is valid, i.e. that the CA signature is correct, that the 'chain of trust' leading up to higher-level CAs is intact, and that it is not expired or revoked. The relying party also needs to check the conditions for use of the certificate. These obligations are often referred to as "relying party obligations". Some of the checks needed to fulfil these obligations can be performed automatically – for example software can verify the expiry date of the certificate.

The relying party in a PKI can be the same party as the one issuing the certificates (the CA). This is e.g. the case in many e-banking solutions where the bank is the CA but also the party that relies on a signature created by the bank customer (certificate holder).

8.3 Policies and procedures in a PKI

8.3.1 Legal importance

The rules governing the issuing and use of certificates and electronic signatures are vital from a legal perspective. A purely technical PKI without any rules framework does not produce much legal certainty. Most legal issues in connection with digital signatures revolve around enforceability in a court of law and liability of the parties involved. It is of no use being able to prove which private key created a signature, if you cannot be sure who the holder of this key is! It is therefore important to understand the role that policies and procedures play in a PKI.

8.3.2 "Policy-based PKI" – the CP and CPS

The mere fact that you have a certificate issued by a certain CA may be of little value if you don't know anything about the rules and procedures that govern the CA's operations.

The fact that the CA, through its signature on the certificate, tells you that the certificate is trustworthy does not in itself mean much. Certificates can vary significantly, and for good reasons: a certificate that is trustworthy for an email exchange about renting a car may not be trustworthy enough in a contractual negotiation about a major construction project. These are some of the issues that differentiate certificates:

- The CA can be run with more or less technical and operational security.
- The process used to identify the certificate holders can be based on more or less stringent procedures (e.g. check of passport, e-mail address, credit records).
- Keys can be generated, communicated and stored with varying degrees of security. The private key can e.g. be stored or protected only with a password, or alternatively in secure hardware (e.g. on a smart card or USB token).
- The CA can limit the use of certificates and its liability in various ways through contracts, notices etc.
- One CA can issue certificates of various kinds – in some cases ranging from practically worthless to extremely trustworthy.

To add legal certainty to a technical PKI a technique has been developed to help CAs communicate about the strength of their certificates in a standardised manner. At the basis of this technique is a policy (the *Certificate Policy, or CP*), which sets the high-level requirement on the CA's operations. The CA then uses a *Certification Practice Statement (CPS)* to describe how it complies with the policy, as well as different legal documents to bind the different parties to a set of common rules. A CA that uses such an infrastructure will below be referred to as a *policy-based PKI*.

The CP is the highest-level document in a policy-based PKI. Its purpose is to determine the level of trust that the CA strives to provide by setting out *what* the CA should do. A CP may be issued as a series of trust requirements from an organisational user, which the CA has to meet. It does not necessarily prescribe in much detail how this level of trust is to be achieved.

The CPS addresses the way in which a CA meets the applicable CP, i.e. *how* the CA lives up to the CP requirements.

The widely adopted document providing guidance on CPs and CPSs is the Internet Engineering Task Force's (IETF) *Internet X.509 Public Key Infrastructure Certificate Policy and Certification Practices Framework*[19], here referred to as "RFC 2527". RFC 2527 has in November 2003 been replaced with RFC 3647, however the latter document modernises rather than modifies RFC 2527.

8.3.3   Relying party notices and agreements

The CA needs to take care to notify the relying party of the conditions for use of a certificate and the limitations of liability (see further 9.4.2.2 Adequate notice to relying parties below). If adequate notice of essential terms is not given, a relying party may not be deemed to be bound by the terms and conditions underlying the certificate, which in turn can lead to liability for the CA.

The design of most CPs and CPSs does not take account of the fact that most legal systems will not grant legal effect to agreements or notices that are too complex, obscure or voluminous for the circum-

---

19   Internet Engineering Task Force (IETF) *Internet X.509 Public Key Infrastructure Certificate Policy and Certification Practices Framework*, which can be consulted on http://www.ietf.org/rfc/rfc2527.txt.

stances. It is not reasonable to expect, for instance, an individual to wade through a 200-page legal document before deciding to rely on a certificate. Realising this, the Internet Engineering Task Force (IETF) has worked out a standardised short-form notification document called the PKI Disclosure Statement (PDS). The PDS proposes a list of critical issues that a CA needs to notify to relying parties in a relatively short and simple document, including validation procedures used, reliance limits, limitations of liability, certificate status checking obligations of relying parties.

It should be noted that the subject of enforcing rules against relying parties remains an area of divergence, despite the above-mentioned IETF efforts. A complicating factor is that certain PKI implementations lend themselves to a contractual approach by using "agreements" to "bind" relying parties without there being an established contractual relationship. Contractual approaches work well in closed environments, but their value is more limited when parties are not part of a common infrastructure.

8.3.4 Trusting the CA

8.3.4.1 Root certificates and CA chains

We have seen how a CA can use policy-based PKI to create a commercially and legally sound security infrastructure based on public key cryptography. However, the problem remains that anyone with decent technical skills can issue certificates for themselves and everyone else under any name.

The identity of a CA can be *verified by comparing the thumbprint (hash)* of the CA's own certificate with a thumbprint communicated by the organisation operating the CA, e.g. via telephone or other channel. If you want to establish the trustworthiness of a certificate, you can in addition to establishing the CA's identity, read its policies and practices. In many circumstances, this provides a sufficient basis for taking an informed and responsible reliance decision.

Based on these techniques, many CAs function independently as a trusted entity in specific communities. However, as communities grow larger and more diverse, the number of entities trusted by all lower levels decreases. For certain communities and applications, therefore, CAs can have their certificates signed by other CAs. This leads to *chains* of trusted entities, each with an ultimate authority that is sufficiently known and trusted by all certificate holders. An ultimately trusted entity in such a chain is often called a *Root-CA*. Some Root-CAs have their certificates pre-installed in very widely used software components such as browsers and web servers. Such CA certificates are often called *public root certificates*.

When a (Root) CA certificate is installed in widely used and trusted software, one can generally be sure that the identity of the CA organisation has been appropriately verified. However, few software vendors legally accept responsibility for this identification. Strictly speaking, therefore, pre-installed CA certificates can be convenient but they do not in itself provide strong security.

8.3.4.2 Trusted Third Parties

The assertion that CAs must be trusted by all lower levels has given rise to the concept of a *trusted third party (TTP)*. The concepts of CA and TTP are often used interchangeably. This, in turn, has lead some people to believe that a CA, to be reliable, must never issue end user certificates to itself. This is a misunderstanding: there are many scenarios where it is natural (and thus often beneficial for security) for one of the communicating parties to act as the CA. Rather than carrying these sometimes artificial distinctions too far, it is more productive to base the decision to use an external CA or allocate CA responsibilities to one of the communicating parties on a factual comparison between the costs and risks of each solution.

While in the 1990s PKI was expected to quickly allow global interoperability based on hierarchies of trust leading up to globally recognised brands, this has become a reality only for so-called web server certificates used for electronic commerce on the public Internet. For all other PKI applications, the trend today is towards smaller-scale usage e.g. on a country or regional bases or within a defined e-business network.[20]

---

20 See, e.g. the report on the use of electronic identification and signatures by the Swedish Post and Telecom Agency: Post&Telestyrelsen, *Användningen av elektronisk identifiering och signaturer*, PTS-ER-2004:3 2004, pp. 16, 26.

8.4   Legal aspects of electronic signatures

8.4.1   Legal certainty

Much of the trustworthiness of an electronic signature depends on the degree to which participants can rely on it to *enforce their legitimate rights* in a court of law. In other words, it is determined by the degree to which electronic signatures can be backed up with *legal certainty*.

One reason why policy-based PKI is the preferred technology for electronic signatures is that the system is built to "incorporate enforceability", by supporting authenticity, integrity and non-repudiation. Although there is normally nothing to prevent the parties from entering into an agreement by exchanging emails that contain the parties' respective names at the bottom, and although such a typed name will in many jurisdictions be considered an electronic signature, it can be difficult to enforce such a contract if either party tries to repudiate it. The reason is that the email signature does not ensure authenticity, integrity or non-repudiation, but is easy to forge.

When an electronic signature is dependent on an identity assertion from a third party (the CA in a PKI), the *liability* issue becomes another aspect of legal certainty. The aim of policy-based PKI is that any reasonably acting party (see next section) who relies on a digital signature, has the ability to *enforce a signature* against a signer or, should this not be possible, to *recover damages* from the issuing CA. It should be noted, though, that just as in most other cases in real life there is no such thing as perfect legal certainty; indeed there can be cases where a reasonably acting relying party remains 'stuck' with damages.

8.4.2   Reasonable reliance

Although PKI can be said to "incorporate enforceability" it is important to understand that one cannot blindly rely on a digital signature. Before having the options to enforce a certificate or invoke a CA's liability, a relying party has to take certain steps to assure itself of the certificate's validity and appropriateness. These measures are often referred to as *relying party obligations*, and having taken these steps means that you are *reasonably relying* on a certificate (see Obligations of the relying party below). The other side of the coin is the CA's notification of the conditions of use of a certificate (see 8.4.2.2 Adequate notice to relying parties below).

8.4.2.1 Obligations of the relying party

Before relying on a certificate the relying party must take certain steps to verify the trustworthiness of a certificate[21]:

1 Check the certificate's *validity*, which means that the relying party has to check that the certificate
   a) has been *signed by the CA* and that the "chain of trust" to any higher-level CAs is intact;
   b) has *not expired*;
   c) has *not been revoked*.

   The above checks are typically performed automatically by the relying party's verification software.

2 Respect any *usage restrictions* and *liability limitations* adequately notified (see 9.4.2.2 Adequate notice to relying parties below), or other conditions for use of the certificate, e.g. in the CP or CPS. In some cases, this more normative reliance decision can be semi-automated: the software can be programmed to accept only certificates governed by rules previously judged appropriate by a human being.[22]

If the relying party has not taken these steps, it cannot be said to *reasonably rely* and may as a consequence not be able to enforce a certificate or invoke the CA's liability. As an example, if the relying party has relied on a signature based on a revoked certificate without having checked its revocation status, the relying party cannot hold the certificate holder responsible for the signature, nor can it hold the CA liable – had the relying party been "reasonable" and checked the revocation status, it would never had relied on the signature.

---

21 *See* relying party obligations in United Nations Commission on International Trade Law (UNCITRAL), UNCITRAL Model Law on Electronic Signatures with Guide to Enactment, 2001, found at http://www.uncitral.org/english/texts/ electcom/ml-elecsig-e.pdf ("UNCITRAL Model Law on Electronic Signatures"), Article 11(b); in American Bar Association (ABA), *Digital Signature Guidelines (with comments)*, 1996 section 5.4 (found at http://www.abanet.org/scitech/ec/ isc/dsgfree.html); and in ETSI *Qualified Certificate Profile, ETSI TS 101 862* section 6.3.

22 Such reliance is then based on an Object Identifier (OID) which identifies a particular policy.

8.4.2.2   Adequate notice to relying parties

The CA needs to take care to notify the relying party of the conditions for use of a certificate and the limitations of liability.[23] Meaningful notification of terms and conditions is a key requirement in contract law. It is even more important in non-contractual situations such as those between a CA and a relying party in complex e-business scenarios. The adequacy of a CA's notice of essential terms in its CP and CPS to a large extent determines the effectiveness of a policy-based PKI.

The certificate itself has very limited space for including contract terms. Often the certificate only includes a reference to a CP and CPS, where the full terms and conditions can be found. This way of introducing conditions via reference is called "incorporation by reference". Normally this must be done in a conspicuous and clear manner in order to be legally valid.[24] When assessing the appropriateness of a notification, it is not only the conspicuousness of the reference that is taken into account but also the accessibility of the document referred to as well as how perspicuous the terms and conditions are.[25]

In the following sections we assume that the relying party has acted reasonably when making its choice to rely on the certificate.

8.4.3   Enforceability

A prerequisite for enforcing an electronic signature in a court of law is that the judge admits it as evidence and considers the signature to have legal effect.

---

23   The UNCITRAL Model Law on Electronic Signatures states that the CA shall give the relying party a possibility to ascertain limitations of liability, Article 9(1)(d)(iv). Limitations according to the E-Signature Directive should be done in the certificate in a way that makes them recognisable to third parties, Articles 6(3) and 6(4).

24   The UNCITRAL Model Law on Electronic Commerce with Guide to Enactment, 1996, with additional article 5 bis as adopted in 1998, note 16, found at http://www.uncitral.org/english/texts/electcom/ml-ecomm.htm ("UNCITRAL Model Law on Electronic Commerce") Article 5 bis states that information should not be denied legal effect solely on the grounds that it is incorporated by reference in a data message.

25   Udsen, Henrik, *Den digitale signatur – ansvarsspörgsmål*, pp. 234.

8.4.3.1 Form: Admissibility as evidence

Before reviewing the quality of an electronic signature, a judge has to decide whether the signature is at all admissible as evidence. This is matter of procedural law. Most laws today accept the admission of electronic data, including electronic signatures, as evidence in court. This is often ensured by a rule that prohibits denial of admissibility solely because the signature is in electronic form.[26]

8.4.3.2 Legal effect

Once a signature has been admitted as evidence, the judge has to decide whether the signature has "legal effect".

Non-discrimination of electronic signatures

Just like e-signature laws today include a non-discrimination rule regarding the admissibility as evidence of the signature, they also include a non-discrimination rule on the legal effect, which typically states that an electronic signature should not be denied legal effect only because it is in electronic form.[27]

However, the non-discrimination principle does not necessarily mean that the judge will find the signature sufficiently trustworthy to enforce. The judge further has to assess the probability that the signature was the result of an error or fraud. If the judge deems it sufficiently probable that the certificate was indeed validly issued to the named end entity, then the relying party may enforce the signature. The non-discrimination rule does thus not mean that all electronic signatures are enforceable, but only that they should not be turned down *only* because they are electronic – they may still be denied legal effect because they are not sufficiently secure.

---

26 *See e.g.* the E-Signature Directive Article 5.1; UNCITRAL Model Law on Electronic Commerce Article 9 and Uniform Electronic Transactions Act, 1999 National Conference of Commissioners on Uniform State Laws (NCCUSL) ("UETA") Section 13.

27 In jurisdictions with freedom of evidence an explicit provision of non-discrimination is normally not needed.

Equivalence to handwritten signatures

In some cases there are in law requirements that something be signed with a handwritten signature (a so called "form requirement"). In such cases an electronic signature may in some jurisdictions be able to meet this requirement, whereas in others this is not possible. However also in states where form requirements generally can be met with electronic means, there may be exceptions to this principle. In areas such as real estate law and family law it is seldom possible to substitute an electronic signature for a handwritten signature. Certain laws have introduced specific kinds of electronic signatures to meet requirements for handwritten signatures, such as the *qualified electronic signature* in the EU Directive on Electronic Signatures[28] (the "E-Signature Directive").

8.4.4   Non-repudiation

With the functions authenticity and integrity it is possible to establish the source of a message, and that the message has not been changed after it was signed. This makes it difficult for the purported signer to later deny that he or she signed the message – it is difficult for him or her to "repudiate" the message.[29] In order to strengthen the non-repudiation a time-stamping mechanism can be used. If it can be established at what time a signature was made, it will be more difficult for a purported signer to claim that he or she was not in control of his private key at the time of the signing.

However, the technical notion of non-repudiation is not the same as the legal. Data that is deemed non-repudiable from a technical perspective may still be possible to repudiate from a legal point of

---

28 Directive 1999/93/EC of the European Parliament and of the Council of 13 December 1999 on a Community framework for electronic signatures.
29 Technically non-repudiation (of origin) is defined as a service intended to protect against the originator's false denial of having created the content of a message and of having sent a message. The ISO standards also include a wider notion of non-repudiation, which is a service is intended to collect, maintain, make available and validate irrefutable evidence concerning a claimed event or action in order to resolve disputes about the occurrence or the non-occurrence of the event or action. *See* ISO/IEC 13888-1: Information technology – Security techniques – Nonrepudiation- Part 1: General: 1997 and ISO/IEC 10181-4: Information technology – Open Systems Interconnection – Security frameworks for open systems: 1997.

view, and vice versa. The legal notion of non-repudiation does not only rely on technology, but also takes account of the behaviour of the parties and other circumstantial aspects. A correct implementation of the technical standards thus does not prevent a party from effectively repudiating a message or a signature, e.g. due to lack of intent. A technical implementation that does not benefit from non-repudiation as technically defined may still not be possible to legally repudiate, due to other factors that may prove that the signer intended to be committed by the signature.[30]

8.4.5 Liability

8.4.5.1 Certificate holder liability

When talking about liability in a PKI the focus is normally on the CA's liability.[31] However, it should be noted that the certificate holder can also be liable for damages.

The CA and the certificate holder have a contractual relationship where both parties can be liable for breach of contract if they don't comply with their respective obligations.

Between the certificate holder and the party relying on a certificate there may or may not be a contract. In a non-contractual situation the question is what happens if the relying party is prejudiced due to the certificate holder's negligence in e.g. protecting its private key. There are good reasons to protect the relying party in case the certificate holder has been negligent, an approach that certain laws have adopted.[32] Many e-signature laws do not deal with certificate holder liability, in which case the answer will need to be sought in national tort law.

---

30 It has been discussed what legal value a certificate's key usage setting for "non-repudiation" has. *See e.g.* Winn, Jane K., *The Emperor's New Clothes: The shocking truth about digital signatures and internet commerce*, 37 Idaho L. Rev. 353, 2001.

31 For a thorough analysis of the liability aspects of digital signatures, with special focus on Danish law, *see* Udsen, Henrik, Den digitale signatur – ansvarsspörgsmål (Copenhagen 2002).

32 According to the UNCITRAL Model Law on Electronic Signatures Article 8.1(a) the certificate holder shall exercise reasonable care to avoid unauthorised use of its private key.

8.4.5.2   Basis for CA Liability

As explained above, the CA is responsible for registration of the key holder, the issuing of certificates and for publishing certificate revocation information. As the core of a PKI it is important to understand to what extent the CA will be liable towards certificate holders and relying parties that suffer loss due to faulty CA-services.[33]

The most obvious situation is when the certificate incorrectly identifies the holder of the certificate, and a relying party due to this cannot enforce a signature based on that certificate. Another case is when a third party has gotten hold of the private key and the relying party cannot enforce a signature purportedly made by the certificate holder.

The basis is that the CA is liable for loss caused by the CA, if the CA has been negligent in performing its obligations. The CA does thus not have a "strict" liability (liability for all damage suffered by the certificate holder or relying party, regardless of the CA's own fault).[34]

CA liability varies depending on jurisdiction, but as explained above the CA can generally be said to be liable if it is negligent (does not take *due care*). The content of notions such as due care and negligence also varies per jurisdiction, and, e.g., the E-Signature Directive contains a presumption that the CA is liable unless it proves that it was not negligent.[35]

CA liability in a policy-based PKI is typically a function of the CA's own communicated policies and practices, unless the law includes minimum requirements and obligations of a CA.[36] A good illustration of CAs' due care obligations is the "key-binding" process: the CP and the CPS respectively prescribe and describe the way in which the key binding is effected. Thus, if mistakes are made in this process (e.g. the wrong person is identified due to lack of prescribed identity-check) that the CA should reasonably have prevented (i.e. the CA is negligent), the CA will be liable for loss suffered.

---

33   If a CA has outsourced the registration process to an RA, the RA will normally be considered as part of the CA from a liability perspective.
34   Such a liability has been discussed based on analogies with electronic payment methods, but dismissed due to basic differences in the systems, Udsen, Henrik, Den digitale signatur – ansvarsspörgsmål, pp. 161–162.
35   E-Signature Directive Article 6.
36   ABA, Digital Signature Guidelines, comment 1.8.2.

However, in order to further refine this model of PKI-based legal certainty, the CA can also take steps to mitigate its own liability risk. In this context it is important to understand the difference between contractual and non-contractual liability.

8.4.5.3 Contractual liability

Contractual liability concerns the liability between parties of an agreement. In situations involving ordinary business use of PKI, parties are generally free to regulate liability in their agreement in any way they see fit. In so-called closed systems, where the CA has agreements with all the parties in the PKI, the CAs will thus often use contracts to limit their liability.[37]

8.4.5.4 Non-contractual liability

For certificates used outside well-controlled closed e-business environments, it is often impracticable or even impossible for the CA to create valid contractual relationships with all potential relying parties. In the absence of a valid agreement, the legal relationship and liability between the CA and relying parties is thus regulated by the law. In such circumstances, the CA's liability is strongly influenced by the degree to which a CA can effectively inform a relying party of key legal issues included in its CP and CPS – this problem is usually referred to as that of *adequate notice* (see above 9.4.2.2 Adequate notice to relying parties).

8.4.5.5 Limiting liability

Most jurisdictions allow the CA to limit its liability, although there may be restrictions as to how far such limitations can be enforced. There are different ways to limit liability: by a limitation of the transaction value for which a certificate can be used, by restricting the area of use for the certificate, by imposing an aggregate liability "cap" per certificate etc. The CA must give the relying party *adequate notice* of

---

37 In certain jurisdictions there are mandatory laws that restrict the CA's possibilities to limit its liability (see e.g. further regarding the EU E-Signature Directive below under Liability).

such limitations. This is often done by effectively communicating relevant rules in the CP and CPS, or in a contract, if applicable.

When damage is caused by acts or omissions that are due to "gross negligence" or wilful misconduct most jurisdictions will not allow the CA to limits its liability, no matter how explicit the notification is. Limitation of liability is further often restricted towards weaker parties, such as consumers. As we will see below some laws explicitly restrict the CA's possibilities to limit its liability.

8.5 E-signature legislation in Europe and elsewhere

8.5.1 From technology specificity toward neutrality and general legal acceptance

Governments started recognising the potential of PKI for enhancing trust in electronic communications in the beginning of the 1990's. Digital signature laws emerged from the mid 1990s,[38] but while PKI was generally considered the most appropriate technology for electronic signatures, the technology specificity of the digital signature laws was criticised. It was argued that by focusing on one technology, the law would become obsolete as technology evolved. This led to a change in the legislative approach and a more technology neutral legislation became the focus.[39] However, despite this change in concept today's legislation is in many cases not really technology-neutral. Often the regulation aims at PKI but the digital signature terminology is replaced with more technology-neutral terms.[40]

---

38 Utah Digital Signature Act from 1995 was the first regulation of digital signatures. Illinois Electronic Commerce Security Act from 1998 regulated both digital and electronic signatures. See also Washington Electronic Authentication Act, Missouri Digital Signatures Act and Minnesota Electronic Authentication Act.

39 The UNCITRAL Model Law on Electronic Signatures removed the notion of "enhanced electronic signatures" from the drafts and now deal with electronic signatures. Also the political process leading up to the EU E-Signature Directive replaced the term "digital signature" used in early drafts with the more technology neutral "electronic signature".

40 *See e.g.* the EU E-Signature Directive where the early drafts included "digital signatures", but were later modified to deal with "electronic signatures", although digital signatures obviously stood model for the "advanced electronic signature". For a comparison of e-signature laws *see* Mason, Stephen, *Electronic Signatures in Law*, LexisNexis Butterworths, 2003.

Electronic signature legislation generally aims to ensure legal recognition of all electronic signatures and to ensure equivalence between electronic and handwritten signatures, in some cases with presumptions for certain PKI-based signatures. Since 1995 all the world's leading trading nations have adopted or are in the process of adopting legislation rendering electronic signatures legally acceptable. These legislative efforts can be divided into three different approaches.

a) General recognising legislation which aims to ensure that electronic signatures are not denied admissibility as evidence or legal effect and that they can be used to meet form requirements (e.g. for handwritten signatures), e.g. the US legislations Uniform Electronic Transactions Act ("UETA") and the US Electronic Signatures in Global and National Commerce Act ("E-Sign Act").

b) PKI-specific legislation, which is normally more detailed and also deals with liability issues, e.g. Japan's law on Electronic Signatures and Certification Authorities and Russia's law on Electronic Digital Signatures.

c) A combination of the above, which includes some general provisions, but also some PKI-specific ones, including liability, e.g. the EU E-Signature Directive and the UNCITRAL Model Law on Electronic Signatures.

8.5.2 Standards and the law

As we have seen, digital signature implementations to be meaningful must get both the technical and legal aspects right. Many of the technical and related legal issues around PKI have benefited from a high level of standardisation. These standards can have real legal implications; industry standards that have developed over a long time are often seen as an expression of current practice and thus considered to represent a "norm" for a certain sector or area. An example of legal relevance of a standard is when assessing whether someone has been negligent – if a party has followed a standard (e.g. RFC 2527) a judge will likely presume that it was not negligent.

> Bodies developing and publishing authoritative PKI-related standards include the IETF (Internet Engineering Task Force) at the international level and CEN (European Committee for Standardisation) in the EU.

There is another way that standards may take on legal importance, and that is by the law making a reference. An example is the E-Signature Directive that authorises the EU Commission to establish and publish certain standards. Such standards have been drafted by the EESSI (European Electronic Signature Standardisation Initiative). Meeting such standards entails a presumption that the applicable requirements of the E-Signature Directive have been met, although nothing prevents a party from meeting those requirements in another way.

8.5.3   UNCITRAL and other international fora

At a global level harmonisation efforts have been led by the United Nations Commission on International Trade Law (UNCITRAL).[41] In 1996 UNCITRAL adopted a Model Law on Electronic Commerce[42] that has become the basis for much of the worldwide e-commerce and e-signature legislation. The Model Law on Electronic Commerce does not specifically regulate digital or electronic signatures, but includes more general rules that can be helpful in signature use. The basis is a so-called "non-discrimination rule" according to which information should not be denied legal effect solely on the ground that it is in the form of a data message.[43] This is also called the "functional-equivalent" approach, which is based on an analysis of the purposes and functions of the traditional paper-based requirement with a view to determining how those purposes or functions could be fulfilled through electronic commerce techniques. The model law further provides that a signature requirement in law can be met in relation to a data message if a method is used that is as reliable as was appropriate for the purpose. Such method should identify the signer and also indicate the signer's approval of the information.[44] The law also includes a provision that a data message

---

41   See http://www.uncitral.org/en-index.htm.
42   United Nations Commission on International Trade Law (UNCITRAL), UNCITRAL Model Law on Electronic Commerce with Guide to Enactment, 1996, with additional article 5 bis as adopted in 1998, note 16, found at http://www.uncitral.org/english/texts/electcom/ml-ecomm.htm.
43   UNCITRAL Model Law on Electronic Commerce Article 5.
44   UNCITRAL Model Law on Electronic Commerce Article 7.

should not be denied admissibility in legal proceedings on the sole ground that it is a data message.[45]

In order to give further guidance on the issue of electronic signatures, UNCITRAL went on to develop a Model Law on Electronic Signatures.[46] It re-states the rule from the Model Law on Electronic Commerce whereby an electronic signature can meet a requirement for a signature in law.[47] This is a very flexible and technology-neutral provision, whereby any electronic signature that is "sufficiently reliable" in a particular situation can validly replace a handwritten signature. The Model Law on Electronic Signatures further establishes a presumption that a signature with technical features corresponding to those of a digital signature shall be treated as equivalent to a hand-written signature.[48] Still without mentioning the words PKI or digital signature, the model law includes basic rules of conduct that may serve as guidelines for assessing liability for the CA, the certificate holder and the relying party.[49] The Model Law on Electronic Signatures has however not found universal acclaim and has not been used as the basis for legislation to the same extent as the higher-level Model Law on Electronic Commerce.

The International Chamber of Commerce's (ICC) guidance document General Usage for International Digital Electronic Commerce (GUIDEC) includes best practice guidelines for authentication of messages and management of digital certificates.[50]

Although the American Bar Association is not an international organisation they have reached some international status through their Digital Signature Guidelines, which aim to establish best practices for digital certificates and signatures.[51] The ICC GUIDEC is largely based on the American Bar Association work in this area.

---

45 UNCITRAL Model Law on Electronic Commerce Article 9.
46 United Nations Commission on International Trade Law (UNCITRAL), UNCITRAL Model Law on Electronic Signatures with Guide to Enactment, 2001, found at http://www.uncitral.org/english/texts/electcom/ml-elecsig-e.pdf.
47 UNCITRAL Model Law on Electronic Signatures Article 6.1.
48 In an effort to be technology neutral the term digital signature is not used. UNCITRAL Model Law on Electronic Signatures Article 6.
49 UNCITRAL Model Law on Electronic Signatures Articles 8, 9, 11.
50 International Chamber of Commerce (ICC), *General Usage for International Digital Electronic Commerce (GUIDEC)*, 2nd Edition 2001, http://www.iccwbo.org/home/guidec/guidec_two/foreword.asp.
51 See American Bar Association (ABA), *Digital Signature Guidelines (with comments)*, 1996 http://www.abanet.org/scitech/ec/isc/dsgfree.html.

8.5.4   EU

8.5.4.1   The Directive on Electronic Signatures

The E-Signature Directive[52] was adopted partly in reaction to national legislative efforts around e-signatures carried out in certain European countries during the latter half of the 1990's. These national legislations were perceived as possible obstacles to e-commerce within the Internal Market. The purpose of the E-Signature Directive is 1) to facilitate the use of electronic signatures and to contribute to their legal recognition and 2) to open the European market for electronic signatures and certification services. In addition to rules on legal effect and liability as will be dealt with below, the E-Signature Directive addresses, *inter alia*, voluntary accreditation and supervision of CAs.[53]

8.5.4.2   Electronic signatures and their legal effect

Electronic Signature

An electronic signature according to the E-Signature Directive is "data in electronic form which are attached to or logically associated with other electronic data and which serve as a method of authentication". This is a very broad definition covering both a digitised image of a handwritten signature as well as a digital signature, and meant to be able to cover also future technologies for authenticating data.[54]

The E-Signature Directive includes a non-discrimination rule that states that electronic signatures may not be denied legal effectiveness or admissibility as evidence in legal proceedings solely on the grounds that it is in electronic form or that the signature in question is not a so called *Qualified Electronic Signature*.[55]

---

52 Directive 1999/93/EC of the European Parliament and of the Council of 13 December 1999 on a Community framework for electronic signatures.
53 *See The Legal and Market Aspects of Electronic Signatures* for a thorough analysis of the E-Signature Directive and its implementation.
54 The term "electronic signature" relates to "data authentication" and does not cover methods and technologies for "entity authentication", *see The Legal and Market Aspects of Electronic Signatures*, p. 27.
55 The E-Signature Directive Article 5.2.

Advanced and Qualified Electronic Signatures

The E-Signature Directive further defines a second level of electronic signature, the so-called *Advanced Electronic Signature*. An *Advanced Electronic Signature* is an electronic signature that is:

1 uniquely linked to the signatory;
2 capable of identifying the signatory;
3 created using means that the signatory can maintain under his sole control; and
4 linked to the data to which it relates in such a manner that any subsequent change of the data is detectable.

The requirements are formulated in a technology neutral way, although in practice they refer to digital signatures. The E-Signature Directive does not give these Advanced Electronic Signatures in themselves any legal effect, but use the definition as a basis for legal effect of what is commonly referred to as *Qualified Electronic Signatures*.[56] Such Qualified Electronic Signature is an Advanced Electronic Signatures based on a *Qualified Certificate* and created with a *Secure Signature Creation Device*. For these kinds of signatures the Member states must ensure that they:

a) satisfy the legal requirements of a signature in relation to data in electronic form in the same manner as a hand-written signature satisfies those requirements in relation to paper-based data; and
b) are admissible as evidence in legal proceedings.[57]

This means that where in relation to paper documents a handwritten signature would have been sufficient, Member States have to give an equivalent status to *Qualified Electronic Signatures* when they start to allow the use of electronic data as a substitute for the paper documents. It is important to remember though that a *Qualified Electronic Signature* is not a synonym for "legally valid electronic signature" – rather, member states are not allowed to require more secure or burdensome signatures to fulfil handwritten signature requirements.

---

56 The E-Signature Directive does not use this term, but many member states do in their implementation of it.
57 The E-Signature Directive Article 5.1.

The E-Signature Directive includes requirements in its Annexes for, *inter alia*, the *Qualified Certificate* and the *Secure Signature Creation Device*. CEN (European Committee for Standardisation)[58] and ETSI (European Telecommunications Standards Institute)[59] have within the EESSI (European Electronic Signature Standardisation Initiative)[60] developed standards on the basis of the requirements of the Annexes to E-Signature Directive. These standards are presumed to meet the Annexes' requirements.

8.5.4.3 Liability

The E-Signature Directive includes liability provisions for issuers of Qualified Certificates, when such certificates are issued to the public.[61] There are no liability rules in the E-Signature Directive for other types of certificates or electronic signatures.

As a minimum Member States must ensure that the CA is liable for the damage caused to any entity which reasonably relies on a Qualified Certificate, unless the CA can prove that it has not acted negligently. This is a presumption rule which means that if damage is caused by the specific circumstances laid down in the E-Signature Directive, then the CA will be presumed liable without the damaged party having to show that the CA was negligent. Note however that the relying party cannot just blindly rely on a certificate – there is a reasonableness requirement inserted in the law (see Reasonable reliance above).

The CA can limit the extent to which the certificate can be relied on by restricting the use of the certificate and limit the value of transactions for which it can be used. These are the only ways in which the CA can limit its liability. The E-Signature Directive does not allow the CA to limit the damage to a pre-determined amount (a so called liability cap). In order to limit its liability the CA must ensure that the relying party is duly notified (see 9.4.2.2 Adequate notice to relying parties above) of the restrictions and limitations.

---

58   http://www.cenorm.be/cenorm/index.htm.
59   http://portal.etsi.org/Portal_Common/home.asp.
60   http://www.ict.etsi.fr/EESSI_home.htm.
61   The E-Signature Directive Article 6. The E-Signature Directive uses the term Certification Service Provider (CSP) instead of CA.

For this reason the E-Signature Directive prescribes that limitations should be included "in the certificate".[62]

As mentioned above the E-Signature Directive only includes rules on liability for Qualified Certificates issued to the public. For other types of certificates and certificates used in closed communities, the E-Signature Directive is silent.

8.5.4.4 *The E-Signature Directive transposed into national law*

A directive does not automatically have effect in the member states, but needs to be transposed into the member states' national laws. The EU member states had until July 2001 to implement the E-Signature Directive. In 2003 a study was undertaken on behalf of the EU Commission to investigate the results of the implementation.[63] The study showed that the primary aim of the E-Signature Directive, which was to ensure a basic legal recognition of electronic signatures within the EU and allow for the free cross-border flow of signature products and provision of services, had not been fully met. This is believed to be partly due to misunderstandings of the E-Signature Directive in the member states. The study does not recommend amending the E-Signature Directive, due to the cumbersome process that this would entail, but stresses that there is a need for clarification of the E-Signature Directive.[64] Areas that would need to be clarified are, e.g., the purpose of the non-discrimination rule, the purpose and use of *Qualified Electronic Signatures*, as well as the concept of "to the public".

8.5.5 USA

The US, as well as many other common law countries including e.g. Canada, Australia Ireland and the UK, has adopted e-signature legislation based on or influenced by the UNCITRAL Model Law on Electronic Commerce.

---

62 It has been discussed whether this means that the full text must be included in the certificate, or if it is sufficient that the certificate includes a link to the CP or CPS, which includes more information on limitations. Udsen, Henrik, *Den digitale signatur – ansvarsspörgsmål*, p. 223f.
63 *The Legal and Market Aspects of Electronic Signatures.*
64 *The Legal and Market Aspects of Electronic Signatures*, p. 9.

The Uniform Electronic Transactions Act (UETA)[65] drafted by the National Conference of Commissioners on Uniform State Laws (NCCUSL) has been implemented in many US states. It includes a rule on non-discrimination, stating that a signature may not be denied legal effect solely because it is in electronic form. The Act further establishes the equivalency of electronic signatures and manual signatures by stating that an electronic signature satisfies legal requirements for a signature.[66] Execution of wills, codicils and testamentary trusts are, however, exempted.

As for the definition of e-signatures it is "an electronic sound, symbol, or process attached to or logically associated with a record and executed or adopted by a person with the intent to sign the record". Thus no specific technology is needed to create a valid signature, but there needs to be an *intention to sign*. This is the differentiating factor compared to a purely technical use of an electronic signature technology.[67]

The US Electronic Signatures in Global and National Commerce Act[68] (E-Sign Act) is a federal law intended to facilitate the use of electronic communications. It imports many of the provisions of UETA into the federal legislation and does not deviate from UETA in its electronic signature approach. Neither UETA nor the E-Sign Act includes provisions on liability or damages.

8.6 Trends and future of electronic signatures

In the late 1990s, many authoritative writers in the IT industry started to raise the possibility that PKI might never live up to its promise of enabling any-to-any e-commerce over open networks. And yet, few serious people believe there can be a future for information security and electronic signatures without PKI; there are

---

65 Uniform Electronic Transactions Act, 1999 National Conference of Commissioners on Uniform State Laws (NCCUSL).

66 These provisions are based on UNCITRAL Model Law on Electronic Commerce, Articles 5 and 7.

67 Section 2 Definitions, Comment to 7. "Electronic Signature", Uniform Electronic Transactions Act, 1999, with Prefatory Note and Comments, National Conference of Commissioners on Uniform State Laws (NCCUSL) 1999.

68 Public law 106–229 Electronic Signatures in Global and National Commerce Act, 2000.

---

simply no real alternatives for it. If it is so useful and unique, how-ever, then why does it take so long for the world of IT to use it to its full potential? One reason lies in the fact that PKI is by definition a multi-disciplinary technique and requires the contribution of law-yers, engineers and businessmen. In addition, the first PKI solution vendors adopted strongly proprietary approaches, which have hin-dered the development of interoperability – one of the prerequisites of productive PKI.

One way to look at the development of PKI is through analyst firm Gartner's concept of a "hype cycle": promising new technolo-gies first have to go through an unproductive hype and then through a period of disappointment before their potential can be fully exploited. In hype cycle terms, PKI plumbed the "trough of disillusionment" by the turn of the millennium. Since then, new business and legal approaches, standards and technologies have emerged that give PKI a renewed chance to be a powerful enabler of electronic transactions.

A factor that has played a role in the continued push towards the development of workable PKI models has been the world preoccu-pation with security and corporate governance that has marked the beginning of this millennium. The dreadful events of September 11 in the US and a raft of corporate scandals have lead to a new term, "information assurance", to describe what is needed to bring IT practices to a level where all players can be subject to appropriate controls and responsibilities. PKI and digital signatures must play a key role in achieving information assurance, however a (healthy) trend can also be observed towards viewing PKI for what it really is – not a "silver bullet" technology but a *risk management technique*. As such PKI needs to be applied in an appropriate manner and in com-bination with other technologies to produce its benefits. Building on generic e-signature legislation aiming to facilitate the recogni-tion of electronic signatures, new laws with information assurance obligations are now being enacted. The full impact of these laws has not yet been realised by economic actors in most geographies, but the coming years can be viewed as critical in the evolution of PKI and digital signatures.

For PKI's renewed chance to be fully realised, future develop-ments in law and standardisation need to incorporate technical, legal and other expertise in a more balanced manner. Practice would also benefit from a higher level of recognition that PKI technology can be used for varying and essentially very different purposes, and that use for achieving legal effect is – especially compared to use for security purposes – in its infancy. Furthermore, to fulfil the promise of new standards and technologies that allow better integration between PKI and normal software functionality, software and PKI vendors need to collaborate to make the PKI "disappear". This incorporation of PKI technology has long been predicted but is in reality far from completed. Finally, these developments will only realise the expected benefits if the integration if based on a holistic system development approach. These efforts and other should go together with a heightened awareness of basic issues, rights and responsibilities in relation to digital signatures.

9 Dispute resolution on the Internet – particularly in auctions and exchanges online

Christina Ramberg

9.1   The importance of preventing disputes

It is interesting how rarely legal disputes in courts concern auctions and exchanges, considering the long history, the many transactions, the speculative element and the large amounts involved. Auctions and exchanges appear to be transactional procedures which discourage disputes. It is wise to create the same feature when the transactions are made electronically.

The explanation for the infrequency of disputes is probably that most auction markets and exchanges require participants to be familiar with the marketplace procedures. Many exchanges and commodity marketplaces only admit bidders and invitors after extensive years of apprenticeship or examinations ensuring that the participant is familiar with the rules of the marketplace. Furthermore, the 'social pressure' in a traditional exchange or auction is strong: participants acting against the rules and traditions can immediately feel the irritation of the other participants in the room.

The features of education and social pressure in a traditional marketplace are not always present in an electronic marketplace. There are frequently no access restrictions that ask about familiarity with the 'rules of the game' and the social pressure is not as strongly felt in the electronic environment. There is also the fact that it is difficult to ensure that participants have read and understood the procedural regulations in the membership terms and conditions of sale.

It is clear that most participants are unlikely to take the time to read the terms and certainly will be unable to fully understand the consequences. This leads to a possible risk that electronic auctions and exchanges will be more litigious than physical auctions and exchanges have been.

The technical design may to some extent prevent disputes. It is essential that the technology implemented by the marketplace guide the participant's behaviour in the appropriate directions by, for instance, making it technically impossible to announce a withdrawal when withdrawal is not permitted. Furthermore, the technology should be secure and unambiguously show – openly or only to the marketplace administrators – from whom a bid is coming and make it impossible to submit bids at the same moment. Another technological feature used in order to limit misunderstandings and mistakes is that the system provide 'warning boxes' when a participant is acting strangely compared with his previous behaviour or general participants' behaviour.

9.2 Institutionalised arbitration, ad hoc arbitration and mediation

Many disputes can be prevented by transparency, education and efficient technology. However, disputes are not wholly unavoidable. Thus, the marketplace needs an efficient mechanism for dispute resolution.

9.2.1 Permanent Arbitration Board

Many traditional auctions and exchanges have their own dispute resolution institutes. In the electronic environment it is highly recommended that specialised arbitration boards be established that are permanently connected to the marketplace. Frequently, traditional trades offline already have special dispute resolution institutes (see for instance auctions for the sale of wool in Australia and tea auctions in London) that can be connected to an Internet marketplace. The benefits of a permanent dispute resolution board are that the arbitrators can be chosen from a pre-set list of experts; this is time-efficient and ensures that the arbitrators are familiar with the type of transaction in dispute. Furthermore, such a scheme normally ensures that the dispute is handled immediately and in a rather formalised manner.

9.2.2   Ad hoc arbitration

The arbitration could be of an ad hoc nature, with the board of arbitrators specifically appointed at the time a dispute occurs. The disadvantage is that the place and procedures of the arbitration must either be specified in the membership terms and conditions of sale or refer to national legislation on arbitration. Furthermore, it can be time-consuming and costly to appoint ad hoc arbitrators when disputes arise rather frequently, i.e. there might be scale efficiency in establishing a permanent dispute resolution board.

9.2.3   Institutionalised arbitration

In marketplaces where the frequency of disputes is not large enough to justify a permanent resolution board, it is possible to tie the marketplace to a general institute of arbitration.

9.2.4   Mediation

It is not advisable for auction or exchange marketplaces to set up mediation schemes. This has become quite a popular way of solving disputes, but it is not well-suited for auctions or exchanges. In auctions the parties make quick transactions and there is generally volatility in the market with varying prices. It is thus important that the decisions in relation to disputes are made quickly. Furthermore, the need for strict compliance with the 'rules of the game' points to the desirability of unambiguous allocation of responsibility and a high degree of foreseeability. The outcome of mediation, where the parties are often involved in a vague process of give and take, is generally hard to predict. Furthermore, the result of mediation does not normally provide guidance for other participants on how to behave in the future. Another reason why mediation is not appropriate for auctions and exchanges is that parties involved in speculative transactions are not as likely to reach an agreement under which they renounce their legal rights.

9.3 The risk of partiality

A particular problem arises when the dispute is between a participant and the marketplace operator as opposed to a dispute between two participants. If the arbitrators are chosen from a list provided by the marketplace operator, there is an obvious risk of partiality. The arbitrator may – due to self-interest – be inclined to favour the marketplace operator in order to be retained on the list of arbitrators.

For such disputes it could be advisable to refer to an unbiased arbitration institute, such as the International Chamber of Commerce International Court of Arbitration in Paris[1], the American Arbitration Association (AAA)[2] or the Arbitration Institute of the Stockholm Chamber of Commerce[3]. Some arbitration institutes provide simplified arbitration, which could sometimes be an advisable alternative.

A greater challenge is to create a permanent dispute resolution board with safeguards against biased arbitrators. An example of such safeguards is to allow participants to appoint persons to the list of arbitrators and for an individual dispute resolution system to use a combination of arbitrators appointed to the list by the marketplace operator and by the participants.

9.4 Costs

The cost of the dispute resolution could either be paid by the marketplace or by the loser of the dispute, or else shared equally by the disputing parties. It is important to stipulate in the conditions of sale and the membership terms, in the procedures set up for the permanent dispute resolution board, or in the rules of the arbitration institute, how the costs of dispute resolution are to be allocated.

1   http://www.iccwbo.org.
2   http://www.adr.org.
3   http://www.chamber.se/arbitration/.

9.5 Quick justice as compared to the right to a fair trial

There are two conflicting interests related to the question of how formalised the dispute resolution ought to be. On the one hand, dispute resolution should provide an opportunity to respond extensively to the other party's arguments and to hear witnesses and experts (the right to a fair trial). On the other hand, justice requires that a decision be made quickly (1) in order to avoid one of the parties dragging out the proceedings in order to harm the other party, and (2) so that the cost of dispute resolution can be limited.

In recent years there has been a strong tendency in both court proceedings and arbitration to emphasise the need to respect all procedural elements of a fair trial. In commercial marketplaces, however, the procedure should not be excessively formalistic. Quick justice could be advanced, for instance, by allowing only one written statement from each party. The need to use oral witnesses is normally limited when the dispute arises from an electronic transaction and consequently there is no pressing need for oral proceedings. The emphasis on quick justice is particularly relevant in marketplaces where the transactions are speculative in nature and exposed to rapid price variations.

The electronic business models are often characterised by the increased speed of decision-making. Naturally, decisions taken in auctions and exchange transactions are typically made quickly. The parties need predictability in order to ascertain their level of liquidity and manoeuvring room. They are often helped more by a quick decision as how to allocate the responsibility when something has gone wrong, than by obtaining a perfectly accurate award after a long period of time. Lengthy dispute resolution is not consistent with the business needs of electronic auctions and exchanges. In designing the dispute resolution scheme for electronic auctions and exchanges it is crucial to take into consideration the greater need for quick justice and to find an appropriate balance in relation to the interests of a fair trial. It is not advisable blindly to develop dispute resolution schemes on the basis of the rules for institutionalised arbitration or national legislation on arbitration. Rules for simplified arbitration may serve as a more appropriate source of inspiration.

9.6   Enforcement

The greatest advantage of arbitration is that the awards are enforceable almost everywhere, due to the widespread adoption of the 1958 New York Convention on the Recognition and Enforcement of Foreign Arbitral Awards.[4] So far, it has proved much more difficult internationally to enforce decisions by national courts.

As stated above, disputes arising from transactions made in electronic marketplaces rarely need to be settled by oral proceedings, since witnesses are normally of no importance. It is consequently efficient to conduct the arbitral proceedings online. Under most jurisdictions this is no problem. Requirements for writing and signatures are nowadays frequently explicitly acknowledged in legislation even when made electronically.[5]

The remaining problem is that in enforcing an arbitral award the New York Convention, Article 1 (1) refers to a territory of a state where the arbitral award is made. When the arbitration is made electronically it may be difficult to establish where and in which state the award was made. In non-electronic situations, however, courts have applied this requirement rather non-formalistically. Furthermore, the 1958 New York Convention has a requirement of fair trial and it is uncertain how speedy arbitration can be and still satisfy this requirement.

Enforcement seldom needs help from national authorities. There is mostly a strong incentive on participants to comply voluntarily with arbitration awards produced as a result of a dispute in an Internet marketplace, when the consequence of disobedience is exclusion from further participation. The conditions of sale and the membership terms should contain provisions on the consequences for participants who do not voluntarily adhere to arbitral awards.

---

4   See the Convention and a list of states that have ratified it at http://www.uncitral.org.
5   See for example http://www.ueta.online; Council Directive (EC) 2000/31 on E-commerce; and the UNCITRAL Model Law on Electronic Commerce (http://www.uncitral.org).

9.7   Publication of arbitral awards

The marketplace can choose to make the arbitral award secret or not. It is useful for all marketplace participants to have knowledge of the decisions by the dispute resolution institution, but the disputing parties may wish not to 'wash their dirty linen in public'. In order to meet both these points, the outcome could be published without disclosing the names of the disputing parties. The published awards may be used to show how the conditions of sale and membership terms function in practice. Furthermore, the awards may be used when making revised versions of the conditions of sale and membership terms, and in the education of present and potential participants. Naturally, the published awards may also serve as precedents for future disputes. Publication of arbitral awards helps to limit ambiguities, which ultimately prevents future disputes from arising.

9.8   Effects during the dispute resolution

A general problem is that the situation may become immobilised while the dispute resolution is pending. In order to reduce the losses, it could be decided that as soon as a dispute arises, the auction should be re-opened. When, for instance, the bidder argues that he or she was entitled to the goods at 100 the auction may be immediately re-opened. If the bidder then acquires the goods at the re-opened auction at 120 and eventually wins the dispute, his damage is easily established to be 120–100 (20). If the bidder does not acquire the goods, but somebody else does, the bidder in the dispute could quite easily prove his amount of damages as the balance between 100 and the price the goods was eventually sold for.

As early as 1745 the conditions of sale in book auctions held by Baker said: '… if any Dispute arises, the Book or Books to be put to Sale again.'[6] This is also a common way of resolving disputes today.[7]

---

6   Learmount, B., *A History of the Auction*, Bernard & Learmount, London, 1985, p. 47.
7   Atiyah, PS., *The Sale of Goods*, 9th Edition, Pitman Publishing, 1995, p. 33.

9.9 Arbitration online in business-to-consumer transactions

Much national legislation forbids or restricts the possibility of settling disputes by arbitration outside national courts. At the same time, it is often acknowledged that normal court proceedings are so cumbersome that in practice the consumer is not well protected. For electronic transactions the parties may voluntarily agree on an outside-court-dispute resolution scheme, bearing in mind that according to some national legislation the consumer still retain its right to not adhere to the award but require that the dispute also be tried by the national court. Even if arbitration is not "allowed" in consumer transactions, it is often a good procedure as a first step towards solving disputes.

9.10 Summary

Internet marketplaces are likely to benefit from special dispute resolution schemes. In designing such schemes the following should be taken into account:

1 the type of arbitration;
2 how to avoid partiality in disputes between the marketplace operator and participants;
3 procedures allowing for quick dispute resolution;
4 rules for re-opening the transaction during the dispute resolution phase;
5 how to ensure voluntary adherence to awards;
6 how to ensure enforcement of awards;
7 a policy for publication of awards.

10 Criminal law in an internet environment

Erik Wennerström

10.1 What is IT crime?

The phenomenon here referred to as "IT crime" appears under many names – *computer crime, high-tech crime, and cybercrime* are just three of the most common – which shows that there is no generally agreed definition of the phenomenon. What the different definitions have in common is that they refer to crimes that can be committed in an electronic environment. A distinction is sometimes made between *IT-specific* crimes and *traditional crimes* committed with the *aid of IT*. A functioning reference is *IT crime*, meaning the use of IT and of the Internet and its services as *functions, targets* or *means* in the commission of crime. Although an exhaustive list of the ways in which IT crimes can be committed is theoretically possible to compile at any given point in time, all practical considerations force us to abandon any such attempt, as methods are being developed at such a rate that a new method will probably see the first light of day while you are reading this introduction. In IT jargon more than in legal terms, some of the most prevalent forms of crimes have been given their own names, such as hacking, cracking, spoofing, sniffing, DOS-attacks, computer vandalism, viruses, and Trojans, just to mention a few. The traditional forms of crime that are easily adaptable to the IT environment – the computer-related crimes – include property and economic crimes (misdirecting funds or distorting financial data, stock market manipulation, etc), sabotage, threats, preparation for assault and abuse, telecommunications crimes (such as avoiding charges), credit card fraud, fraud, hate crimes, trade in illegal substances, copyright intrusions, espionage, illegal gambling, embezzlement, soliciting sexual services, and child pornography, as well as all ancillary forms of these crimes.

While several countries around the world have introduced criminal law sanctions against individuals having committed such crimes, IT crimes differ from "normal" crimes in several ways. One way in which they differ from traditional forms of crime is that although certain acts are prohibited by law, the technical complexity of IT makes it hard for most citizens to see where the line between legal and illegal behaviour is drawn. Furthermore, the social stigma linked to traditional crimes (with some variations, e.g. when comparing violent crimes with minor traffic violations) is underdeveloped: IT criminals such as hackers are in some communities actually seen as rebels or even pioneers, and are hailed as such, whereas the stigma of paedophilia is no different online than it is offline.

How big is the problem caused by this sort of crime? Different estimates have been made, one such suggesting that the cost of Internet fraud is expected to reach between US$ 5 billion and US$ 15 billion by 2005.[1] Crime rates are decidedly high: the Internet Fraud Complaint Center (IFCC), a partnership in the US between the Federal Bureau of Investigation (FBI) and the National White Collar Crime Center, received 30,503 complaints of Internet fraud between May 2000 and May 2001.[2] These figures relate to only one form of it crime. Secure information about the costs and size of the total problem cannot be reliably established, but the trends are constantly demonstrating increases. In spite of this, attempts to find robust solutions to the problems of fighting IT crime, have all stumbled on the difficulty of agreeing on language to balance effective law enforcement powers with human rights standards. This is not unique to IT crimes, but perhaps more conspicuous here: any criminalisation will be perceived as a restriction of a liberty and any measure to facilitate law enforcement in IT environments will automatically be accused of infringing everyone's privacy. Any legislative measure will subsequently be seen as a compromise – which they are – and accordingly as far from perfect, on whatever side of the compromise the beholder stands.

---

1   *See* Meridien Research, reported at epaynews.com
    (http://www.epaynews.com/statistics/fraud.html).
2   For more information see
    http://www1.ifccfbi.gov/strategy/IFCC_Annual_Report.pdf.

The starting point in this chapter is the situation in Europe in general, rather than in individual countries, as this balancing act between the interests of law enforcement and the interests of human rights has characterised developments in this region. Most European countries are Member States of the Council of Europe, and 25 of the countries are Member States of the European Union. The activities of those two institutions will be at the forefront in this chapter.

10.2 The crimes

High-tech or cybercrime normally refers to traditional forms of crime committed in the IT environment, such as fraud or forgery, and to a somewhat lesser extent to forms of crime that are unique to that environment, such as *hacking*[3] and *denial-of-service attacks*.[4] The first type of crime is where people lose money directly, whereas the second type may result in losses, but more seldom in money going out from an account. What is perhaps left out in some such references is content-related crimes, such as child pornography or racism, and the infringements of intellectual property rights. Regardless of whether a broad or narrow definition is used, this form of criminality is often transnational – every activity adding up to the completed or attempted crime normally leaves traces in more than one jurisdiction, and the successful investigation and prosecution of such crimes inevitably will require a transnational response. An effective and well-functioning system of international co-operation is vital to that response. Several of these issues have been raised in the context of the United Nations, where the following acts have been identified as requiring criminalisation

- unauthorised access to a computer system
- interference with lawful use of a computer or computer system
- destruction or alteration of data within a computer system

---

3   Unauthorised alterations in a computer program or operative system.
4   DOS-attacks; flooding a system with useless traffic in order to overburden it and thus cause it to malfunction.

- theft of intangible property, and
- obtaining value by deception (including electronic systems). The balance already referred to was underlined there as well, but to date little legislative work has been undertaken in this specific field at global level.[5]

Several of the efforts that have been initiated to create common rules and mechanisms to protect European society from cyber-crimes are now moving on from the negotiation and adoption phase to the implementation phase.[6]

When the Council of Europe concluded the negotiations that led to the Cybercrime Convention,[7] it targets first and foremost the harmonisation of Criminal law. The Convention suggests common elements for criminalisation in all states ratifying the Convention, in three areas of criminal law.[8] The first area is referred to as *crimes against the confidentiality, integrity and accessibility of data and systems*, and covers the crimes of

- illegal access to a computer system,
- illegal interception of data communication,
- data interference in a system,

---

5   See *The Rule of law in the Global Village – Issues of Sovereignty and Universality*, Symposium on the occasion of the signing of the United Nations Convention against transnational organized crime, panel on "The challenge of borderless cyber-crime", Introductory Remarks and Concluding Remarks by the Moderator of the Panel Mr. Hans Corell, Under-Secretary-General for Legal Affairs. The Legal Counsel of the United Nations, Palermo, Italy, Palazzo dei Normanni, 14 December 2000.

6   Wennerström, Erik, *EU-legislation and Cybercrime – A Decade of European Legal Developments*, in Wahlgren, Peter (ed.), *IT-Law*, Scandinavian Studies in Law, Vol. 47, 2004, p. 452.

7   Convention on Cybercrime, ETS No 185, http://conventions.coe.int/Treaty/en/Treaties/ Html/185.htm.

8   All 43 Council of Europe Member States have participated in the negotiations, together with Canada, Japan, South Africa and the United States. The Signatory States are, as of 1 June 2004, Albania, Armenia, Austria, Belgium, Bulgaria, Croatia, Cyprus, Denmark, Estonia, Finland, France, Germany, Greece, Hungary, Iceland, Ireland, Italy, Latvia, Lithuania, Luxembourg, Malta, Moldova, Netherlands, Norway, Poland, Portugal, Romania, Slovenia, Spain, Sweden, Switzerland, former Yugoslav Republic of Macedonia, Ukraine, United Kingdom, Canada, Japan, South Africa.

- system interference when it is the system as such that is being targeted,
- and the misuse of devices, such as software allowing the user to engage in hacking-like activities.

The second area is made up of *computer-related crimes*, where we find the traditional crimes of forgery and fraud, being committed in an IT environment. The third area is *content-related crime*, which consists of offences related to child pornography. The fourth area is *intellectual property crimes*, mainly relevant to infringements of copyrights. The Convention establishes common definitions of these crimes in the cyber environment, and requires the ratifying states to make these crimes punishable by penalties that include deprivation of liberty, as well as calling for judicial co-operation facilities between the participating states to improve their fight against cybercrime. The Convention on Cybercrime entered into force following its ratification on 18th March 2004 by Lithuania, thereby reaching five ratifications, which was the requirement for its entry into force.[9]

The first part of the Convention requires the Contracting States to ensure the criminalisation of certain offences described – first of all crimes against the *confidentiality, integrity and accessibility* of data and systems or computer crimes (i.e. environmentally unique crime types). This part defines illegal access, illegal interception, illegal damaging and alteration of data, system entry as well as illegal use of certain types of equipment. The Convention goes on to describe the crime of illegally accessing a computer system, in whole or in part, as well as illegal or unauthorised interception of non-public transmissions of computer data. The Convention covers the deletion, alteration and suppression of data – a crime referred to as *data interference* – referring *inter alia* to situations where data is made inaccessible to those authorised to access it. Such situations frequently occur when hackers alter the privileges or authorisation

---

9   The starting point of the process that led to the negotiations can be traced back to a series of recommendations adopted by the Committee of Ministers of the Council of Europe – Recommendations No R (85) 10, R (87) 15, R (88) 2, R (89) 9 and R (95) 13 – as well as to Resolutions 1 (97) and 23 (00) adopted by the European Ministers of Justice. See also Wennerström, *EU-legislation and Cybercrime – A Decade of European Legal Developments*, p. 452 *et seq*.

197

levels of computer files. As the text covers alteration of data, most forms of malicious computer viruses will also be covered by it.[10]

Article 5 criminalises serious *system interference*, resulting in hindering a system from performing the functions it was designed to perform. In order for the interference to be criminal, it must be the result of some form of conscious data manipulation, not mere accident. Unsolicited e-mail advertisement or *spam*, cannot be seen as such interferences *per se*, but the distribution of spam may ultimately result in a system (or server) being overloaded, leading to its malfunctioning. In that situation, it may be argued that a system interference has taken place (based upon a *culpa eventualis* evaluation – the perpetrator had no direct criminal intent, but realised the risk of his behaviour and ignored the risk) with results identical to that of a deliberate denial-of-service attack, i.e. the intentional overloading of a system in order to make it malfunction.[11] Article 6 criminalises the *misuse of devices*, a concept directly imported from the United States.[12] Paragraph 1 of Article 6 criminalises the production and dissemination of devices, mainly designed to commit the crimes outlined in Articles 2–5. This includes the dissemination of passwords and other tools to gain unauthorised access to computer systems, provided there is criminal intent on the part of the perpetrator. Possession of such devices is likewise criminalised, provided there is intent demonstrated to commit one of the listed offences.[13]

As regards *computer-related crimes* (i.e. traditional crime types adapted to the IT environment) the convention defines computer-related fraud and forgery in Articles 7 and 8. Although most States already have criminalised the crimes of fraud and forgery as such, these provisions require States to examine their laws to ensure that they apply to IT situations. Computer-related forgery and fraud are two specific kinds of manipulation of computer systems or data,

10 Convention on Cybercrime (ETS no 185), Explanatory Report, p. 61, http://conventions. coe.int/Treaty/en/Reports/Html/185.htm; Wennerström, *EU-legislation and Cybercrime – A Decade of European Legal Developments*, p. 453.
11 Convention on Cybercrime (ETS no 185), Explanatory Report, p. 69, http://conventions. coe.int/Treaty/en/Reports/Html/185.htm. See also Wennerström, Erik, *Europeiskt arbete mot IT-brottslighet*, Europarättslig Tidskrift, 2001, p. 480.
12 Cf. 18USC1029; see U.S. Code Online via GPO Access, "http://www.access.gpo.gov/ UScode/title18/parti_chapter47_.html".
13 Wennerström, *EU-legislation and Cybercrime – A Decade of European Legal Developments*, p. 453 *et seq.*

and the provisions serve to acknowledge the fact that traditional legal provisions are not always suitably adapted or neutral enough to cover new forms of manipulations.[14]

The Convention also covers some *content-related crimes* and requires States to criminalise, e.g., distribution, production and possession of child pornography through the use of computer systems, according to Article 9.[15] This provision criminalises several aspects of child pornography, which in its offline-form already is criminalised in most States:

- the production of child pornography for the purpose of distribution through a computer system
- the 'offering' and making available of child pornography through a computer system
- the distribution or transmission of child pornography through a computer system
- the 'procuring for oneself or for another' of child pornography, i.e. actively obtaining it through e.g. downloading
- the possession of child pornography in a computer system or on a data carrier, such as a diskette or CD-Rom.

Originally racism and xenophobia was also covered by the Convention's provisions on content-related crimes, but during the finalising stages of the negotiations it became clear that it would not be possible for some of the negotiating states to agree upon a text that basically criminalised what their constitutional guarantees for freedom of expression were safeguarding.[16] Finally we also find among the criminal law definitions infringements of copyright and other intellectual property rights, in Article 10 that states are required to criminalise.[17]

States are required to criminalise these acts through the introduction of penal law sanctions that include custodial penalties. Before

---

14 Ibid., p. 454.
15 This Article was later the model for its counterpart in EU legislation, see below.
16 That provision was subsequently taken out of the Convention, and negotiated separately as a Protocol to the Convention, and as such signed – by currently 23 states; no ratifications – in early 2003; see Additional Protocol to the Convention on Cybercrime, concerning the criminalisation of acts of racist and xenophobic nature committed through computer systems, ETS No 189.
17 Wennerström, *EU-legislation and Cybercrime – A Decade of European Legal Developments*, p. 454 *et seq*.

it is possible to say whether these provisions actually create a finely woven web of substantive criminal law over the ratifying states, it is necessary to see *how* the ratifying states implement them in their national laws. The states are given room for manoeuvre in the implementation, as a result of the compromises that lay behind the text ultimately adopted.[18] Article 11 (3) may serve as an example of how much is still at stake, as it makes the obligation to criminalise the *attempt* to commit the crimes described in Article 2–10 optional for the ratifying states. This may lead to future difficulties regarding, *inter alia*, the requirements for dual criminality.[19]

The possibilities for creating and implementing legislation are naturally greater in the EU, consisting as it does of 25 states already linked together by a vast common legal system of Community law, than among a larger and more loose-knit circle of countries, such as the Council of Europe. The EU being the political union between the states also joined in the EC, "EU" and "EC" normally covers the same phenomenon, and only in a legal sense is it important to distinguish between the two; the EU is based upon the Treaty on European Union (TEU) whereas the EC is based upon the Treaty establishing the European Community (TEC), which is a completely different set of rules. Whereas the Council of Europe is restricted to using the Convention as the instrument for legal harmonisation among its member states – a convention is a inter-governmental agreement that first has to be adopted unanimously and signed by all states concerned, and then ratified by their respective parliaments before it can have any binding effect upon the states and their citizens – the EU has more robust instruments at its disposal, such as EC regulations, adopted through a qualified majority-voting procedure and, without any additional measures being required, directly applicable in all Member States and their courts in the same way as national laws, and EC Directives, which are adopted as regulations and normally applicable in all Member States but stating an objective to be achieved while leaving the Member States to adopt measures they consider necessary for that achievement – and EU framework decisions – very similar to directives, but having their

18 Ibid., p. 483.
19 Ibid., p. 455.

legal basis in the TEU, not the TEC, and following the procedures and logic of that treaty.[20] The EU Commission's first legislative proposal in this field concerned measures against credit card fraud or fraud and forgery of non-cash means of payment, on which the Commission took action as early as 1998, although the Council did not conclude its deliberations until 28th May 2001, when the Framework Decision on Combating Fraud and Counterfeiting of Non-Cash Means of Payment was adopted.[21] This instrument applies to pre-paid and other paper instruments as well as all electronic instruments and applications. Member States are required to ensure criminal sanctions against fraud and counterfeiting of such instruments, when the acts are offences related to

- payment instruments
- computers
- specifically adapted devices.[22]

It is worth noting that the legal framework emerging in the EU was very much inspired by the Council of Europe Cybercrime Convention. It was partly in the light of that experience that the EU initiated the legislative process on child pornography in 2001, when the Commission presented a proposal for a *Framework Decision* (equivalent to a Directive) *on Sexual Exploitation of Children and Child Pornography*[23]. The Framework Decision, which was finally adopted on 22nd December 2003,[24] contains rules for harmonising national

---

20 There are other instruments available as well, such as recommendations, decisions, conclusions, etc., but the three types mentioned in the text are the instruments used for legal harmonisation.
21 Council Framework Decision 2001/413/JHA.
22 See Article 6 of the Cybercrime Convention above. It is the same US Code Article that has influenced European legislation here. Wennerström, *EU-legislation and Cybercrime – A Decade of European Legal Developments*, p. 457 *et seq.*
23 COM (2000) 854, O.J. C62 E/327, 27.2.2001. The proposal for a Framework Decision, a more directive-like instrument for co-operation and approximation in the area of justice and home affairs, that had been introduced with the Amsterdam Treaty on 1 May 1999, actually followed a Joint Action on the same substance that had been presented in November 1998. Some of the co-operative provisions of that proposal were brought forward in a Council Decision 2000/375/JHA of 29 May, 2000.
24 Council Framework Decision 2004/68/JHA, O.J. L13/44, 20.1.2004.

criminal law provisions that are directly applicable to the on-line environment. Member States are required to ensure that the following acts are punishable when committed intentionally, by physical as well as legal persons:

a) production of child pornography,
b) distribution, dissemination or transmission of child pornography, .
c) making child pornography available,
d) acquisition or possession of child pornography.[25]

As regards physical persons, the offences shall carry deterrent sanctions, including prison sentences. All provisions shall be incorporated in Member States' national law by 20th January 2006.

On 28 November 2001, the Commission presented a proposal[26] for a *Framework Decision on Combating Racism and Xenophobia*, aiming at harmonising Member States' criminal law on such offences and to ensure closer judicial co-operation. The proposal also aims to ensure that racist or xenophobic content hosted outside the EU is subject to criminal sanctions inside the EU. The offences include racism and xenophobia through publicly

- inciting violence or hatred,
- insulting or threatening individuals or groups,
- condoning crimes of genocide, crimes against humanity and war crimes,
- disseminating or distributing such material,
- directing, supporting or taking part in activities of groups active with these offences.

The adoption of this Framework Decision, which has been the subject of a lengthy and difficult negotiation, is expected during 2005.[27]

---

25 Cf. Article 9 of the Cybercrime Convention above.
26 COM (2001) 664.
27 Wennerström, *EU-legislation and Cybercrime – A Decade of European Legal Developments*, p. 463.

In 2002 the Commission proposed a *Framework Decision on Attacks Against Information Systems*,[28] aiming at harmonizing the definitions of crimes in this pertinent area, as well as rules on criminal procedure, bringing cybercrime-fighting within the general procedural assistance regime developed in the EU cooporation in justice and home affairs. The Framework Decision was adopted in 2004, and contains common definitions of *illegal access to information systems*, and *illegal interference with information systems* through sending viruses or deliberately overwhelming an information system (denial-of-service attacks).[29]

The purpose of the Framework Decision is to harmonise the Member States' legislation concerning attacks against information systems and to improve co-operation between judicial authorities. The Framework Decision covers areas also covered by the Council of Europe Convention, but is not as extensive in scope. Article 1 contains definitions of technical terms, such as "computer data", concurring entirely with those of the Convention. Instead of "computer system", which is the term used in the Cybercrime Convention, the Framework Decision uses "information system"; both terms cover individual or connected computing devices, but whereas *computer systems* (Cybercrime Convention) treat data in any form, *information systems* (Framework Decision) are limited to handling computer data, which in turn is defined in Article 1 (b). The provisions on illegal access to information systems in Article 2, match Article 2 of the Convention. Paragraph 2 provides Member States with the option to limit the definition of criminal activity to the intrusion through a security device, which is an option also found in the Convention. Articles 3 and 4 on illegal system interference and illegal data interference largely correspond to Articles 5 and 4 in the Convention, see chapter 2 above. Article 5 penalises the dependent

---

28   COM (2002) 173.
29   Cf. Articles 2–6 of the Cybercrime Convention above. Wennerström, *EU-legislation and Cybercrime – A Decade of European Legal Developments*, p. 463.

forms of crime, instigation, aiding, etc. (The Convention covers some of these forms, but has no provisions on instigation.)[30]

Article 10 deals with Member States' jurisdiction: a Member State has jurisdiction over crimes committed on the territory of that State or by one of its citizens abroad. Acts committed on the territory of a State shall also include acts directed towards information systems in another State, as well as acts directed towards information systems in the State by an attacker elsewhere. The jurisdiction provisions state that Member States shall be competent to prosecute

- persons physically present on their territory who attack information systems located in another country,
- persons physically present in another country who attack an information system located on their territory.

Provisions for conflicting jurisdictions and the traditional *aut dedere aut judicare* provision – meaning "either extradite or adjudicate", binding states to either prosecute an alleged offender who is within its territory or to extradite the offender to another state for prosecution there –normally found in EU instruments are also covered in Article 10.

Under Article 11, Member States shall use available co-operation networks for the exchange of information concerning the investigation of the crimes concerned. (Such networks exist on the basis of a multitude of instruments; central authorities, networks of contact points, members of the European Judicial Network, the national prosecutors serving on EUROJUST (the EU prosecution unit) etc.) For co-operation purposes, each Member State shall establish a permanent operational point of contact to facilitate exchange of information on cybercrime attacks. The article refers to "contact points," which is a way of linking the networks together along the same lines as the Convention does through Article 35, i.e. the G8-inspired 24/7-network (see below). Illegal interception, misuse of devices, content-related crimes, computer-related fraud and forgery, as well as rules on criminal procedure and co-operation are not found in

---

30 Ibid., p. 463 *et seq.*

the Framework Decision. Whereas such provisions were needed in the Convention, the EU already has a regime in place covering some of those provisions, namely its mutual legal assistance instruments.[31]

10.3 The procedures

To successfully fight cybercrime, as with any other type of crime, the law enforcement community must be able to investigate, collect evidence, and build winnable cases against the criminals in question. Law enforcement must be able to convince a court of the facts of the crime, demonstrated by evidence. Evidence looks different for different forms of crime; in a murder case there will be a body and a possibly a weapon, in economic crimes there will be a paper trail or not, in burglary cases there will be an illegal entry. With IT crimes, what can be proved is often not manifestly criminal in itself; information passing one way through cyber space will be perfectly legitimate, whereas information taking another route may constitute a serious crime. The information will be binary – 1s and 0s, not blood stains or weapons with fingerprints on them. How does the prosecution make a court see the difference?

Prosecutors may be able to bring in experts to explain the details, but they must themselves have a minimal understanding of the technology behind the acts in order to make legal sense. The tools available to the prosecutors and other law enforcement officials are the procedures for investigating IT crimes, and they differ greatly between nations. The legislators, in most countries, do not necessarily have an understanding of the technical issues, which will affect the tools available on the books. The Council of Europe Convention,

---

31 Most notably in the largely unratified, but most influential Council Act of 29 May 2000 establishing in accordance with Article 34 of the Treaty on European Union the Convention on Mutual Legal Assistance in Criminal Matters between the Member States of the European Union, hereinafter MLA Convention 2000. OJ C 197, 12.07.2000. For a full picture of the mutual legal assistance regime, see e.g. Thunberg Schunke, M, *Internationell rättslig hjälp i brottmål inom EU*, Effektivitet v. rättssäkerhet (International Judicial Assistance in Criminal Matters within the EU. Efficiency v. Legal Certainty), Iustus Förlag AB, Uppsala, 2004; Wennerström, *EU-legislation and Cybercrime – A Decade of European Legal Developments*, p. 464.

however, contains rules, drafted by IT crime experts, on criminal procedure such as coercive measures to facilitate investigations of the crimes described above, through a combination of "old" and "new" procedural measures. One such new measure is the "rapid freezing" of data (including traffic data; see below) i.e. an authority with relevant competence shall have the right to order data concerning a crime or a criminal to be stored with an Internet Service Provider (ISP) in order for it to be deliverable to the investigating authority upon a subsequent formal request for its release. This measure may remain in place for a maximum of 90 days, according to Articles 16–17. Traditional possibilities for search and seizure in order to obtain stored data are provided for in Article 19. Authorities shall have the possibility to secure seized data and to make it inaccessible for unauthorised persons.[32]

The type of data that is normally of high interest to law enforcement purposes is traffic data, i.e. the data generated at the ISPs as a result of their clients' use of their services. Traffic data normally encompasses location data, subscriber data, user data, which together constitutes the data making it possible to trace and identify the source of a communication which includes personal details, contact information and information identifying services subscribed to, to identify the routing and destination of a communication, to identify the time and date and duration of a communication, and to identify the telecommunication. This is how the issue appears in the EU (see more below); in the Council of Europe Cybercrime Convention however, traffic data is defined in Article 1 as "any computer data relating to a communication by means of a computer system, generated by a computer system that formed a part in the chain of communication, indicating the communication's origin, destination, route, time, date, size, duration, or type of underlying service." "Historic" or *ex ante*-traffic data refers to traffic data generated up to a point in time at which a search is made retrospectively, i.e. what traffic data has been generated by a particular client account during the past specified number of months. This type of search would require guaranteed retention of traffic data and

---

32 Convention on Cybercrime (ETS no 185), Explanatory Report, pp. 200–202, http:// conventions.coe.int/Treaty/en/Reports/Html/185.htm. Wennerström, *EU-legislation and Cybercrime – A Decade of European Legal Developments*, p. 455.

will not be possible to conduct with support of the Council of Europe Convention's provisions; only *ex post*-traffic data or data generated in relation to a particular account from a specific point in time (the time when the decision to disclose data, or to grant a request to freeze data, is made) and onwards. The Council of Europe-mechanism is therefore more of a surveillance mechanism for preservation of traffic data than a useful tool for investigating crimes that have already taken place, as law enforcement agencies only in exceptional cases know beforehand who is going to commit a specific crime.

Although excluding historical traffic data, the Convention provides that data shall be presented to the law enforcement authorities at their legally authorised request, in order to identify the operators and the route that particular data has taken in transmission. It shall also be possible for authorities to order an ISP to reveal information on its user/client accounts. The Convention stipulates that it shall be possible for authorities to collect traffic data in real time – again: not going back in time, but from onwards from a certain point in time – that is related to certain data communications, and ISPs may be ordered to assist authorities in relation to such measures. Just as in the offline situation, it shall be possible for authorities to use telecommunications-interception in real time when investigating serious crimes, according to these provisions (Articles 20 and 21). These measures may only be taken under special conditions such as authorisation by a judge or another independent authority, subject to the rules of the Signatory States on human rights and proportionality.[33]

The European Union has to date made few harmonisation efforts in the area of procedural law, but relies here instead on various measures for mutual assistance and mutual recognition of the procedural decisions taken in each Member State.

10.4 Co-operation

It goes without saying that crime fighting in the area of IT crime depends upon co-operation between the law enforcement agencies of

---

33   Ibid. p. 455 et seq.

different countries; at the click of a button, an incriminating package of information can shift location from one jurisdiction to another and defy traditional forms of law enforcement. Co-operation between states to fight cybercrime presents several challenges: what is criminal in one state is not necessarily so in another, and there may be restrictions on authority to act when a matter is not exclusively domestic. The formalities of co-operation may be time-consuming, not adapted to the speed at which cybercrimes are committed and permitting its traces to disappear. Difficulties can also arise when law enforcement activities have extraterritorial effects, which is the case when data going between two or more jurisdictions is intercepted. An issue closely linked to international co-operation and international agreements is subsequently international jurisdiction, as a state's exercise of criminal jurisdiction is ultimately determined by international law.[34]

The Council of Europe Convention's rules on international co-operation aim at making the procedural rules described above enforceable transnationally, by providing possibilities for law enforcement authorities (prosecuting, crime investigating and police authorities) in one state to seize computer-based evidence on behalf of the authorities in another country, Article 31, swiftly and in a less formalised manner in urgent cases, Article 29. The assistance may consist in freezing and seizing in another state certain data that is relevant to an investigation. Central authorities shall be appointed for sending and receiving requests for such assistance, but it shall be possible in urgent cases for authorities to communicate directly with each other. Requests may be refused only under certain circumstances and certain user limitations may come into play as a result of states' rules on data protection. Apart from this, spontaneous and voluntary exchange of information is foreseen.[35]

---

34 See The Rule of law in the Global Village – Issues of Sovereignty and Universality, Symposium on the occasion of the signing of the United Nations Convention against transnational organized crime, panel on "The challenge of borderless cyber-crime", Introductory Remarks and Concluding Remarks by the Moderator of the Panel Mr. Hans Corell, Under-Secretary-General for Legal Affairs. The Legal Counsel of the United Nations, Palermo, Italy, Palazzo dei Normanni, 14 December 2000.
35 Wennerström, *EU-legislation and Cybercrime – A Decade of European Legal Developments*, p. 456.

Pending a formal request for assistance, states shall freeze stored data on request, for at least 60 days. The grounds for refusal are limited. States naturally have the right to access publicly available information without the permission of other states, should the location of such data be hosted on servers there. On request states shall assist each other with real-time collection of targeted traffic data, Article 33 – "targeted" collection as opposed to "fishing expeditions" where, for example, all traffic data generated at a particular server is monitored indiscriminately – for all crimes falling under the Convention, in accordance with the conditions and procedures described in national law. States shall furthermore assist each other with interception of telecommunications as far as is possible with regard to existing treaties and national law, Article 34.[36]

The crimes described in the convention shall be extraditable, according to Article 24, provided that they are punishable with imprisonment for one year or more, with certain exceptions, and that requirements of dual criminality, where applicable, are satisfied.[37] In order to provide support to ongoing investigations, a network of contact points is created, available 24 hours a day, seven days a week, as outlined in Article 35. This network is modelled on the G8 network (see below) and in reality means that the G8 network is expanded to all ratifying States of the Council of Europe convention.[38]

The European Union has not created a special regime of rules for procedural aspects of IT crime; this is mainly left to the Member States. For co-operation the EU relies instead upon a general regime for mutual assistance in criminal matters, the *MLA* regime.[39] Some of the Member States have, however, proceeded in other fora, such

---

36 Idem.
37 This is not a new rule, but basically just an extension of existing rules on extradition – the Council of Europe Convention of 1957 on Extradition, as well as the two EU conventions of 1995 and 1996 – to this convention, which can also be said about the convention's rules on search and seizure in computer environments.
38 See p. 298, Explanatory Report to the Council of Europe Cybercrime Convention. See also Wennerström, p. 456 *et seq.*
39 See Council Act of 29 May 2000 establishing in accordance with Article 34 of the Treaty on European Union the Convention on Mutual Legal Assistance in Criminal Matters between the Member States of the European Union, hereinafter MLA Convention 2000. OJ C 197, 12.07.2000.

as the Council of Europe and the G8. In 1997 agreement was reached within G8's[40] crime fighting activities (the co-operation that is commonly known as the Lyon-group, where the Commission takes part as a representative of the EU as such) on an action plan on high-tech and computer-related crime. This action plan contains several of the actions that have later been transposed into provisions of the Council of Europe Convention (such as the 24/7-network) and into Commission initiatives (such as encouraging special police capabilities for fighting this type of crime). The G8 1997 Action Plan on Combating Cybercrime contains the following points:

1 using established network of knowledgeable personnel to ensure a timely, effective response to transnational high-tech cases and designate a point-of-contact who is available on a 24-hour basis;

2 taking appropriate steps to ensure that a sufficient number of trained and equipped law enforcement personnel are allocated to the task of combating high-tech crime and assisting law enforcement agencies of other states;

3 reviewing G8 legal systems to ensure they appropriately criminalise abuses of telecommunications and computer systems and promote the investigation of high-tech crimes;

4 considering issues raised by high-tech crimes, where relevant, when negotiating mutual assistance agreements or arrangements;

5 continuing to examine and develop workable solutions regarding: the preservation of evidence prior to the execution of a request for mutual assistance; trans-border searches; and computer searches of data where the location of that data is unknown;

6 developing expedited procedures for obtaining traffic data from all communications carriers in the chain of a communication and to study ways to expedite the passing of this data internationally;

---

40 Since 1975, the heads of state or government of the leading industrial democracies USA, Canada, Japan, United Kingdom, Germany, France and Italy have met annually to deal with the major economic and political challenges of the day. From 1994, the G7 – as it then was – met with Russia in connection with each summit and from 1998 Russia participates fully. For more information, see the G8 information centre at the University of Toronto, http://www.g8.utoronto.ca.

7 working jointly with industry to ensure that new technologies facilitate our effort to combat high-tech crime by preserving and collecting critical evidence;

8 ensuring that G8 can, in urgent and appropriate cases, accept and respond to mutual assistance requests relating to high-tech crime by expedited but reliable means of communications, including voice, fax or e-mail, with written confirmation to follow where required;

9 encouraging internationally recognised standards-making bodies in the fields of telecommunications and information technologies to continue providing the public and private sectors with standards for reliable and secure telecommunications and data processing technologies;

10 developing and employing compatible forensic standards for retrieving and authenticating electronic data for use in criminal investigations and prosecutions.

The most tangible result of the G8 action plan is the establishment of a network of law enforcement contact points for combating cybercrime, accessible 24 hours a day, seven days a week, the 24/7 network. This network makes it possible to swiftly and without bureaucracy request assistance from other participating states, in investigations with links into other countries. From the outset the idea was to expand the membership of the network beyond the G8-states, and the network now holds over 30 participating states.[41]

When G8 met in October 1999 to follow up the action plan, one could, apart from the progress made above all in relation to the network, note that the greatest challenge consisted in identifying and tracing criminals in the on-line environment. For this reason certain principles were adopted, on trans-border access to stored data, amounting to rapid freezing of data at the request of another state, simplified mutual assistance and a general permission to access pub-

---

41 EU Member States that had not joined the G8-network have been encouraged to do so, through statements and formal Council Recommendations of the EU. See Council Recommendation of 25 June 2001 on contact points maintaining a 24-hour service for combating high-tech crime. OJ C 187/5, 3.7.2001. Wennerström, *EU-legislation and Cybercrime – A Decade of European Legal Developments*, p. 458 *et seq.*

licly available material in another state, without specific permissions. These principles can now also be found in the Cybercrime Convention, which demonstrates how much cross-fertilisation took place between these processes.[42]

10.5 Enforcing the law

Criminal investigations is an area, where a range of specific problems present themselves. The first problem we note is the limited availability of specialised IT-crime units. Even if such units are available, they may not have the powers to investigate the content of a computer system against the will of a right holder. If a search is nevertheless authorised, encryption may still render the investigation futile, as may legislation in place. The formal requirements regarding the use of electronic data as evidence present a fragmented picture – what would be admissible in one jurisdiction may be entirely inadmissible in another.[43] What the individual – be it a victim, a system administrator or an in-house IT lawyer – has to consider as regards preparedness either to launch an internal investigation or to assist law enforcement authorities in conducting an investigation into an incident, is a multitude of aspects. Anyone responsible for the security of a system, be it ever so small, is wise to have established contact with the local police before any incidents have occurred, in order to establish contact and procedures for reporting incidents should they occur. If the local police have IT competence, it may be prepared to offer advice on how to prevent disasters and also on how to act when disaster strikes.

As a rule, any system administrator is wise to ensure a proper level of logging events in the system; to not log is to ensure that nobody – not on the inside nor on the outside – will ever leave any digital

42 The Commission also noted the concrete measures promoted within the G8, as it formulated its own ambitions in this field. Ib. p. 459.
43 See The Rule of law in the Global Village – Issues of Sovereignty and Universality, Symposium on the occasion of the signing of the United Nations Convention against transnational organized crime, panel on "The challenge of borderless cyber-crime", Introductory Remarks and Concluding Remarks by the Moderator of the Panel Mr. Hans Corell, Under-Secretary-General for Legal Affairs. The Legal Counsel of the United Nations, Palermo, Italy, Palazzo dei Normanni, 14 December 2000.

fingerprints in the system. A suitable level of logging is hard to establish and normally requires adjustments from time to time, as too much logging is not desirable for reasons linked to system capacity and performance. Even with a good level of logging, log files should never be regarded as corresponding to the truth, as the first thing a decent hacker will do upon entering a system is to manipulate its logs and clocks. (In the logging adjustment cycles, it may be opportune to include the rotation of log files, and to synchronise all system clocks.)

If an attack nevertheless occurs, the system administrator can make the subsequent legal proceedings a lot easier if every measure is properly documented, including the nature of the problem, when and how it was discovered, the action taken to save the system and the costs incurred (this is of utmost importance for later being able to make a civil claim for damages). The first priority, regardless of whether we a looking at an internal investigation or a law enforcement investigation, is to "freeze" the situation in the system as close as possible to the time of the incident. This is best done by creating a total backup of the system, preferably by making a mirror copy of the system for forensic purposes, including all sectors of the disc in question. Should that not be possible, a regular backup will be of great assistance too. The affected disc may then be extracted for further analysis, which means that the investigation can be conducted with the original disc as the starting point.

One advantage of involving law enforcement authorities at an early stage in an investigation is the domestic instruments of coercion at their disposal. When following a trace via telecom providers and ISPs, the investigator will normally be asked for a court order, subpoena or other domestic disposition before information is supplied. When the trace leads to investigation abroad, it becomes even more of a challenge without the assistance of law enforcement authorities; the international and regional systems of co-operation and mutual assistance are only available to state actors. It may at first be difficult to decide if there is need for police investigation, or if the internal investigation is sufficient. The prudent course is to always expect that the police will later be involved in the case. As this means that our original disc may later become evidence in a criminal procedure, internal investigations should never analyse an original disc directly, unless it is decidedly so that there will not be any law enforcement investigation later; destroying evidence is actually a crime in itself in several jurisdictions, and even if that should not be the case, it will not serve the victim's interests if information that later becomes part of a police investigation has been affected by the victim's own investigations.

In several countries there are specialised departments (at local, regional and/or national level) that are experts on matters related to IT crime and it may ultimately be such a department that will investigate a reported IT crime. The first contact should, however, be through the normal procedures for reporting crimes. (Companies concerned about publicity that still wish to go ahead and report a committed crime to the police, may be wise to leave out sensitive company information in the first report to the police.)

National police agencies and their specialised IT units can get some assistance from INTERPOL, which has staff specialising in this field, although hardly sufficient to make up for deficiencies in the law enforcement agencies of its member states[44]. Again, the European integration has proved capable of establishing bodies for the purpose of strengthening co-operation between its members, and to some extent add resources at central level. When the mandate of EUROJUST, the unit for co-operation between prosecution services, was formulated, it came to include cybercrime,[45] and when the *European Arrest Warrant* (EAW) – one of the most revolutionising instruments in the history of European judicial co-operation – was drafted, cybercrime was in the list of crimes (together with non-cash fraud and forgery) for which the EAW could be used.[46] Other EU

---

44   Interpol – the International Criminal Police Organization – has its headquarters in Lyon, France. Interpol's mission is to support all organisations, authorities and services whose mission is preventing, detecting, and suppressing crime. Interpol provides three core services to its members, the more than 120 states who are Interpol members, namely a unique global police communication system, a range of criminal databases and analytical services, and support for police operations worldwide. In order to fulfil its mission, Interpol also provides information exchange, platforms for international co-operation, as well as co-ordination of joint operational activities of its member countries. For more information, see http://www.interpol.int.

45   See Article 4 in Council Decision of 28 February 2002 setting up Eurojust with a view to reinforcing the fight against serious crime.

46   See Article 2 in Council Framework Decision (2002/584/JHA) of 13 June 2002 on the European arrest warrant and the surrender procedures between Member States.

bodies have been inspired by this ambition and it should be noted that EUROPOL, the European police office, has established a High-tech Crime Observatory.[47]

The EU Commission proposed in 2003 the creation of the *European Network and Information Security Agency*, ENISA[48]. The purpose of ENISA is to develop expertise to stimulate co-operation between the public and private sectors, provide assistance to the Commission and Member States in their dialogue with industry when addressing security-related problems in hardware and software products. ENISA will also follow the development of standards, promote risk assessment activities as well as interoperable risk management routines and produce studies on these issues.[49]

Just as the Commission in its legislative proposals tries to strike a balance between crime fighting and data protection, the greatest challenge today for the EU is still to introduce far-reaching rules on data protection, while simultaneously increasing the efforts to fight cybercrime. The Commission published a proposal on 12th July 2000 for a *Directive on the treatment of personal data and the protection of privacy in the field of telecommunications*[50]. Until then, the treatment of personal data and protection of privacy had been regulated through a general data protection Directive (95/46/EC) and a special telecommunications Directive (97/66/EC) that deals with issues specific for this sector. Through the new Directive concerning the processing of personal data and the protection of privacy in the electronic communications sector,[51] which was adopted on 12th July, 2002, the "old" telecommunications Directive was updated in accordance with developments in the field of communications and

47 See EUROPOL Annual Report 2002, Council doc. 8578/03 EUROPOL 15, together with EUROPOL Work Programme 2004, Council doc. 8580/03 EUROPOL 17. Wennerström, *EU-legislation and Cybercrime – A Decade of European Legal Developments*, p. 461.
48 The legislative instrument for establishing ENISA is a Regulation (460/2004) adopted on 10 March 2004, on the basis of a proposal of the Commission, doc. COM (2003) 63. See http://www.enisa.eu.int.
49 Wennerström, *EU-legislation and Cybercrime – A Decade of European Legal Developments*, p. 462.
50 COM (2000) 385.
51 Directive 2002/58/EC of the European Parliament and of the Council of 12 July 2002 concerning the processing of personal data and the protection of privacy in the electronic communications sector (Directive on privacy and electronic communications).

technology. The new Directive is accordingly not limited to telephony and computer networks, but also covers satellite, ground carried and digital TV, regardless of which information is going through the systems. The Directive requires service providers to take measures to guarantee the security of their services, as well as the confidentiality of communications and traffic data. Member States are required to ensure that illegal interception, storage or surveillance of communications or traffic data is prohibited. Furthermore, the Directive contains rules on location data, i.e. data indicating a terminal's geographical location. Such data may only be treated with the user's consent or when the data has been depersonalised.[52]

The most important issue in this context concerns traffic data, i.e. the data generated when transferring messages and information between two addresses on the networks. According to the main provision in Article 6 of the Directive, traffic data must be erased or made anonymous as soon as the transmission of data has been concluded, except when it is needed for billing purposes or, with the consent of the subscriber, value added-services. In the latter situation the service provider must inform the subscriber of the types of traffic data that will be treated and how long the treatment will go on. The thrust of the article is that all information about the addresses between which communication has taken place is erased the moment transmission is concluded, which means a period of a few minutes at most.[53]

Article 15 permits exceptions to the main rule in Article 6, e.g. for purposes relating to national security and law enforcement. National interception rules can subsequently be used, as they will break through the data protection rules. Articles 6 and 15 could, however, if used in isolation, create a situation where traffic data could be observed *ex post* only, from the moment a decision is taken that certain communications shall be intercepted; all relevant traffic data before that point in time would have been erased or made anonymous. Should a denial-of-service attack take place, all communications preceding the attack will be out of sight and what happens after the attack has been discovered (i.e. when the system has

---

52 Wennerström, *EU-legislation and Cybercrime – A Decade of European Legal Developments*, p. 465.
53 Idem.

collapsed) is presumably of little relevance. The possibilities for the police to seek the assistance of a service provider in tracking a picture containing child pornography figuring in a chat room on the Internet, would likewise be reduced to nil, since there are no longer any traces of the communication from the moment the picture has been sent to the chat room; we would know that the picture is there but not how or from where it got there. All will depend on how these national rules of exception are formulated.[54]

The implementation of the Directive into national laws will require co-ordinated action of the national measures concerning crime fighting – should the Directive be implemented in different ways in this respect in the different Member States, it will create a situation where some Member States will be able to co-operate to fight certain crimes, whereas others will find that they have sacrificed the safety of their citizens on the altar of data protection, turning ISPs on their territory into havens for computer criminals.[55]

Following the adoption of Directive 2002/58/EC on the processing of personal data and the protection of privacy in the electronic communications sector, the Member States were required until 1st July 2003 to implement its provisions, whereas the optional possibility for Member States in article 15 to limit that obligation for purposes of, *inter alia*, national security and law enforcement, can be utilised at any time after that implementation deadline as well. (Needless to say, a Member State having once permitted its ISPs to not retain traffic data will face a steeper challenge when later introducing such obligations, than a Member State with such provisions already in place.)[56]

The possibility in Article 15 comes with a qualification, namely that any restrictions of the application of article 6 must be such that they are "necessary, appropriate and proportionate measure within a democratic society ...". Ultimately only the European Court of Justice can interpret the scope of this qualification, and it is likely to do so only if and when a Member State or a body of the EU – normally the Commission – brings a charge of infringement against a Member State or the Council before it. When Member States make

54   Ibid., p. 465 *et seq.*
55   Ibid., p. 466.
56   Wennerström, *EU-legislation and Cybercrime – A Decade of European Legal Developments*, p. 466.

217

use of the exception in Article 15, the Member States will not know beforehand if the Commission will charge them with infringement of the EC Treaty, on the grounds that the exception made was too far-reaching in scope (the data to be retained or the purposes for which it should be retained) or in time (the length of the retention periods), in order to qualify as a measure "necessary, appropriate and proportionate measure within a democratic society ..." in the eyes of the Commission and, later, the Court. The only way for Member States to avoid having such a sword of Damocles hanging over their rules of data retention is for the Member States to agree, by means of an EU instrument, on a uniform set of minimum rules regarding the retention of traffic data. During the Danish Presidency over the EU, difficult negotiations finally resulted on 19th December 2002 in a set of Council Conclusions[57] on information technology and the investigation and prosecution of organised crime. These conclusions call for such a joint effort by the Member States to agree upon common definitions of minimum scope and time for traffic data retention for law enforcement purposes.[58]

Following intense and substantive consultations, a *Draft Framework Decision on the retention of data processed and stored in connection with the provision of publicly available electronic communications services or data on public communications networks for the purpose of prevention, investigation, detection and prosecution of crime and criminal offences including terrorism*, was proposed to the Council on 28th April 2004, by France, Ireland, Sweden and the United Kingdom.[59] Article 1 of this instrument outlines the scope and aim of the Framework Decision, which is to facilitate judicial co-operation in criminal matters by approximating Member States' legislation on the retention of data processed and stored by Internet and other telecommunications service providers, for the purpose of prevention, investigation, detection and prosecution of crime or criminal offences including terrorism. The Article underlines that its provisions do not apply to the content of communications, nor to the interception and recording of telecommunications. Article 2 sets the legal

---

57   Council doc. 15763/02.
58   Wennerström, *EU-legislation and Cybercrime – A Decade of European Legal Developments*, idem.
59   Council doc. 8958/04 CRIMORG 36/TELECOM 82.

definitions of the technical terms figuring in the legislative text. The most important definition concerns "data" which refers to data necessary to

- trace and identify the source of a communication which includes personal details, contact information and information identifying services subscribed to.
- identify the routing and destination of a communication.
- identify the time and date and duration of a communication.
- identify the telecommunication.
- identify the communication device or what purports to be the device.
- identify the location at the start and throughout the duration of the communication.

The main provisions of the Framework Decision are found in Article 3, which obliges the Member States of the EU to ensure that data is retained by ISPs, and Article 4, which defines the length of the retention period as at least 12 months and not more than 36 months. (According to Article 4, Member States may have longer periods for retention of data dependent upon national criteria when such retention constitutes a necessary, appropriate and proportionate measure within a democratic society.) A Member State may apply other retention periods as regards Short Message Services (SMS), Electronic Media Services (EMS) and Multi Media Messaging Services (MMS), and concerning Internet Protocols including Email, Voice over Internet Protocols, world wide web, file transfer protocols, network transfer protocols, hyper text transfer protocols, voice over broadband and subsets of Internet Protocols numbers – network address translation data, but for telephony services excluding SMS, EMS and MMS, the retention period suggested in the proposal is non-derogable. Negotiations are in their early stages as this is written, and difficult to predict, but the fact that the Heads of State and Government, meeting in the European Council in Dublin, 25th–26th June 2004, expressed strong support for the draft instrument indicates the political pressure behind the continued negotiations.[60]

---

60 Wennerström, *EU-legislation and Cybercrime – A Decade of European Legal Developments*, p. 467 *et seq.*

10.6 The way ahead

The Council of Europe Cybercrime Convention must, like all conventions, be ratified, a process that can be time-consuming and uncertain – even positive ratifications can be combined with reservations towards certain parts of the agreed text. Herein lays a weakness in the convention as an instrument of legislation, a weakness that is even more evident by comparison with EU instruments (Framework Decisions, Council Decisions, and Directives) that enter into force upon their adoption. According to Article 36, the Convention entered into force when it had been ratified by five states, out of which at least three were member states of the Council of Europe. Lithuania became the fifth country to ratify the Convention and as of 1st July 2004 it is now in force between the states that have ratified it; to date it is not in force in any of the states through which the lion's share of data – legitimate as well as illegitimate – flows. But apart from this the Council of Europe has created an instrument with broad coverage, legally – covering substantive criminal law, procedural law as well as international co-operation – as well as geographically, which is its main advantage.[61] The Convention had great influence well before it entered into force, indeed, even before the text of it had been agreed in 2001, on national, regional and international negotiations and discussions on cybercrime, which demonstrates its unique nature at the time of adoption, and the high technical quality of its provisions.[62]

It is fair to say that the EU is gradually not only catching up with the Council of Europe's extensive convention, but also surpassing it in scope and in strength, utilising the stronger framework for both legislation and for co-operation that the EU provides.[63] Although progress is significant on the substantive criminal law side, it is,

---

61 Albania, Croatia, Estonia, Hungary, and Lithuania were the first five States to ratify the Convention. For these five, the Convention entered into force on 1 July 2004. Romania has since joined the group of ratifying States, and the Convention entered into force in relation to Romania on 1 September 2004. France, Sweden and the United Kingdom are currently in the process of ratifying the Convention.

62 See e.g. references in the explanatory memorandum to the Commission's proposal for a Council Framework Decision on attacks against information systems, COM (2002) 173 final, 19.04.2002. Wennerström, *EU-legislation and Cybercrime – A Decade of European Legal Developments*, p. 457.

63 Ibid., p. 468.

however, impossible to reach the goal (a safer information society) unless the same importance is given to the procedural law issues as has been given to the issues of substantive criminal law. This is the dilemma that the EU finds itself in, having addressed one problem after another which inevitably leads the focus of attention onto crimes and criminalisation efforts, instead of taking the global grip on the problem, as the Council of Europe did, which took some time and had little political appeal in the process. The distance between full protection[64] and the edge of the ongoing legislative processes, oscillates and will continue to do so. If we look at the development in substantive criminal law, we see legislation in place or being prepared (child pornography, racism, hacking etc.) that provides the EU with common definitions which can be superimposed on the definitions gained through the Council of Europe convention. This is clearly raising the common level of protection. Turning to criminal procedural law, however, we see how the Council of Europe Convention introduces an arsenal of important tools for enforcing the law against criminals, albeit not in the most crucial area of traffic data retention, while the EU is still struggling with the paralysis with which its data protection regime creates for law enforcement, or at least did until 11th September 2001. This also affects the possibilities for international co-operation, itself an essential condition for any effective fight against cybercrime.[65]

The European initiatives have succeeded in bringing the substantive criminal laws of the States therein closer together, so that sanctions are at the disposal of all European courts, or will be soon. Measures have also been taken to ensure more effective judicial and police co-operation between the European states. But as long as there is still a question mark over the issue of "fingerprints" – will or will not traffic data be available when a serious cybercrime is investigated? – we cannot be sure whether cases will ever reach a court. In the future, the introduction of broadband technique will increase the volumes of traffic over the IT networks, while making any at-

---

64 Which naturally is an illusion and which should not even be seen as desirable; this is where the Big Brother society lies, not in balancing the needs of law enforcement against the interests of personal integrity, as the recent traffic data initiative demonstrates.

65 Wennerström, *EU-legislation and Cybercrime – A Decade of European Legal Developments*, p. 469.

tempt to monitor that traffic more difficult. Broadband traffic also leaves the individual user more exposed to criminal attacks, as the user is likely to store more information – including banking and other personal information – in the IT environment and spend more time online. This exposure increases even more when combined with wireless networks. Without even adding the challenge of cyber terrorism to the list, it is safe to say that whereas progress has been made in Europe on the legislative side, the challengers to the legislative system are ensuring that the challenges do not end there.

Contributors

Christine Kirchberger, LL.M., Junior Lecturer, The Swedish Law & Informatics Research Institute, Faculty of Law, Stockholm University. Main research areas involve data protection, legal issues regarding digital rights management systems and legal information retrieval. Previous publications include an article on security in electronic public procurement and on information technology for lawyers. She is also the editor of a publication containing Swedish legislation and standard contracts in the field of IT-law (Materialsamling IT-rätt).

Nicklas Lundblad, LL.M. and B.A. in philosophy and literature, Vice President of Stockholm Chamber of Commerce, Sweden. He is a member of the second section of the e-Europe Steering Group, and has participated in a number of European Union expert groups. He is also active in the EBITT-commission in the International Chamber of Commerce, as well as a board member of World Internet Institute in Sweden and ADBJ – the national Swedish organisation for IT and Law. He is also a Ph D Student in informatics working with a research project on the different aspects of technology impact on law. Mr Lundblad has authored two books on information technology, law and society and is a frequent contributor and columnist in a number of Swedish newspapers and magazines.

Cecilia Magnusson Sjöberg, LL.D., Professor of Law and Informatics, The Swedish Law & Informatics Research Institute, Faculty of Law, Stockholm University, Royal Swedish Academy of Sciences Research Fellow. She has had more than 20 years of practical experience of developing and using IT-based legal information systems, including the public and the private sector as well as participation in EU-projects. Major current research project investigates the possibilities of cross-fertilisation of methods for security enhancement and applications of information standards in the legal domain. More information about the SLIM Project (Secure Legal Information Management) is found on www.juridicum.su.se/slim, see also the general homepage www.juridicum.su.se/cema.

Anna Nordén, LL.M., Vice President of Legal and Regulatory Affairs, TrustWeaver AB. Anna has worked internationally in the field of e-commerce and information security at the International Chamber of Commerce (ICC) and the United Nations Commission on International Trade Law (UNCITRAL). She is a board member of the Swedish Society for Computers and Law and chairman of the Swedish Network for E-Business' working group on Law and IT Security. Anna also lectures in IT law at Stockholm University and the Royal Institute of Technology (KTH).

Mikael Pawlo is co-editor of the leading Scandinavian forum on open source and free software (Gnuheter), he is the former Swedish editor of the Nordic Intellectual Property Review, NIR. Pawlo has been an associate at Swedish law firm Lindahl and served on the board of the Swedish Internet industry association, BitoS. Pawlo is currently conducting research in respect of open source legal issues.

Christina Ramberg, LL.D., jur dr Professor of Commercial Law, Göteborg University, Sweden. Ms Ramberg has written extensively about contract law, sales law and e-commerce law. She was for many years Head of the Swedish Delegation in the UNCITRAL Working Group on Electronic Commerce and is presently member of the Coordinating Committee in the Study Group for a European Civil Code.

Erik Wennerström, LL.M., Director International Relations, Ministry of Justice. In the mid-90s he – then as an official of the European Commission – took part in the launching of the EU's initiatives and activities aiming at fighting IT-crime. From 2000, he has been responsible for international IT-security issues at the Swedish Ministry of Justice.

Sanna Wolk, LL.M., is a doctoral candidate at the Faculty of Law, Stockholm University. Current research is within the field of

224

Intellectual Property Law and primarily focus on the rules governing Intellectual Property ownership. She has written a number of academic publications in her research field. Ms Wolk is also the head of four courses at Stockholm University and the Royal Institute of Technology. She is as well a lecturer at Stockholm University, Lund University, Uppsala University, the Royal Institute of Technology and the Stockholm School of Economics. Further on, Ms Wolk is a secretary of a Committee appointed by the Government. The Committee inquires Researchers' Inventions at Swedish universities. She is also Member to the Board of the Swedish Anti Counterfeiting Group, additional member to the Board of the Swedish Association for the Protection of Industrial Property and secretary at the Institute of Intellectual Property and Market Law.

Index